IS-317: Introduction to Community Emergency Response Teams

By

Fema

6/6/2014

Lesson Overview

The Community Emergency Response Team (CERT) Program educates ordinary people about disaster preparedness and weapons of mass destruction. The CERT Program trains you in basic disaster response skills, such as fire safety, light search and rescue, and disaster medical operations. With proper CERT training, you can help protect your family, neighbors, and co-workers if a disaster occurs.

After completing this course, CERT Independent Study (IS)-317, you should be able to:

- Identify key concepts that form the foundation for CERT operations
- Identify principles and guidelines for CERT activities

This lesson provides an overview of the CERT role in disaster preparedness and response. It also covers what you will learn in other lessons about CERT organization and activities.

It should take you approximately **20 minutes** to complete this lesson.

Course Purpose

The purpose of this course is to help you prepare for the classroom-based *CERT Basic Training* course that may be available in your community. This training (WBT) includes many practices useful for dealing with emergencies that may occur in non-disaster situations. The classroom-based training (CBT) includes many additional skills and protocols you can learn through demonstration and hands-on practice in the classroom. Once you successfully complete the CBT, you will be an actual CERT member and will be trained to deal with emergencies that may occur in real disaster situations.

Remember!

You are not a trained CERT volunteer until you have completed the CERT Basic Training classroom course.

Course Structure

The 16 lessons in this course are organized into six modules, to be completed in sequence. Each module is made up of multiple lessons, also to be completed in sequence within each module. The six modules are:

- Module 1: CERT Basics
- Module 2: Fire Safety
- Module 3: Hazardous Materials and Terrorist Incidents
- Module 4: Disaster Medical Operations
- Module 5: Search and Rescue
- Module 6: Course Summary

Now you will have a brief introduction to each module. Are you ready?

Module 1: CERT Basics

In Module 1, you will learn how training as a CERT member allows you to contribute to the safety and welfare of your family and community, and how to prepare your home and workplace for disasters.

There are three lessons in this module:

- **Lesson 1-1: CERT Overview** identifies ways in which you, as a CERT member, can serve your community during emergencies.
- **Lesson 1-2: Family and Workplace Preparedness** will help you prepare your home and workplace for disasters.
- **Lesson 1-3: CERT Organization** shows how CERT organization can provide for your effective participation in disaster response.

It should take you approximately **1 hour 25 minutes** to complete this module.

Module 2: Fire Safety

In Module 2, you will learn the various fire safety practices that CERTs must follow.

There are three lessons in this module:

- **Lesson 2-1: Introduction to Fire Safety** presents the fire safety fundamentals you will need as a CERT member.
- **Lesson 2-2: Fire Hazards in the Home and Workplace** shows you actions that you can take to minimize fire hazards in your home and workplace.

- **Lesson 2-3: Safe Fire Suppression** details actions that CERTs use to suppress fires safely.

It should take you approximately **1½ hours** to complete this module.

Module 3: Hazardous Materials and Terrorist Incidents

In Module 3, you will learn practices that CERTs must follow in situations that involve hazardous materials or terrorism.

There are three lessons in this module:

- **Lesson 3-1: Introduction to Special Situations** details the types of situations that CERTs may face in dealing with hazardous materials and/or terrorism.
- **Lesson 3-2: Hazardous Materials Safety** introduces the actions CERTs take to deal with hazardous materials safely.
- **Lesson 3-3: Terrorism and CERT** discusses protocols you should follow to prepare for a possible terrorist attack.

It should take you approximately **1 hour 5 minutes** to complete this module.

Module 4: Disaster Medical Operations

Module 4 provides an overview of the practices that CERT members must follow during disaster medical operations.

There are three lessons in this module:

- **Lesson 4-1: Introduction to Disaster Medical Operations** identifies the basic principles and practices CERTs need for disaster medical operations.
- **Lesson 4-2: Principles and Guidelines for Survivor Care** introduces key principles and practices CERTs use for medical care of disaster survivors.
- **Lesson 4-3: Disaster Psychology** explains different psychological stresses associated with disaster responses.

It should take you approximately **2 hours 25 minutes** to complete this module.

Module 5: Search and Rescue

Module 5 provides an overview of the practices that CERT members must follow when participating in search and rescue operations.

There are three lessons in this module:

- **Lesson 5-1: Introduction to Light Search and Rescue** presents the key principles and practices that CERTs must follow for light search and rescue operations.
- **Lesson 5-2: Search Operations** introduces practices that CERTs use for safely conducting search operations.
- **Lesson 5-3: Rescue Operations** provides an overview of key procedures that CERTs use for safely conducting rescue operations.

It should take you approximately **1 hour 15 minutes** to complete this module.

Module 6: Course Summary

In Module 6, you'll review the key points you learned in the five previous modules. You'll also learn the steps you must take to receive credit for this based training and how you can download and print your certificate of completion if you pass the test.

It should take you approximately **20 minutes** to complete this module. This does not include time to take the test.

Lesson Summary

In this lesson, you learned that this course:

- Introduces you to basic CERT skills and procedures
- Prepares you for classroom-based *CERT Basic Training* course
- Contains easily navigable features and tools
- Comprises six modules made up of multiple lessons

You have completed this lesson. You are now ready to begin Lesson 1: Introduction to CERT.

Module 1: CERT Basics
Lesson 1-1: CERT Overview

Module Overview

Welcome to Module 1: CERT Basics. In this module, you will learn about the CERT role in disaster preparedness and response. You will also learn the basics about how CERT is organized.

It should take about **1 hour 25 minutes** to complete the three lessons in this module:

- Lesson 1-1: CERT Overview — **25 minutes**
- Lesson 1-2: Family and Workplace Preparedness — **35 minutes**
- Lesson 1-3: CERT Organization — **25 minutes**

After completing this module you should be able to:

- Identify ways in which CERT members contribute to the safety and welfare of their families and communities

Lesson Overview

Welcome to Lesson 1-1: CERT Overview.

After a disaster, emergency responders can become overwhelmed by the needs of their community. Damage to communication and transportation systems often further taxes their resources. It is possible that, following a disaster, CERTs may be called to respond to immediate needs in their area.

This lesson provides an overview of the CERT concept and the ways that CERTs serve as community resources by contributing to emergency preparedness and response.

After completing this lesson, you should be able to:

- Identify ways in which CERTs contribute to disaster preparedness and response

It should take you approximately **25 minutes** to complete this lesson.

CERT Concept

CERT members come from neighborhood, workplace, or other community organizations. Members join because they want to learn how to better prepare for hazards that threaten their homes and communities. They want to protect their families, themselves, and their communities.

The CERT Program began by training community members for earthquake response operations. Under the Federal Emergency Management Agency (FEMA), the CERT Program has grown to cover all types of disasters in communities around the country.

As a CERT member, you will become an active participant in learning about hazards and preparing for them. After training, you may be called upon to support emergency services following a disaster.

CERTs: Community Resource

CERTs are not restricted to disaster-related activities. You have the potential to become a known and trusted volunteer resource in your community. As a CERT member, you can support the response community in many ways. For instance, you can help with community safety projects or help neighbors and co-workers prepare for emergencies.

CERT Participation in Disasters and Emergencies

CERT members have participated in many emergency and non-emergency situations. Here are a few examples of CERT contributions.

Floods - Morgan County, Indiana - June 2008
Massive flooding in central Indiana wiped out 75 percent of farmers' crops and closed a local hospital for five months. Although it took only 8 hours for 11 inches of rain to devastate the area, CERT members were still working six weeks after the storm hit. They performed a variety of jobs, including:

- Handing out food and disaster kits
- Assisting with sandbags
- Directing traffic

Tropical Storm Fay - DeBary, Florida - August 2008
Tropical Storm Fay hit Florida for nearly a week. In DeBary, 22 inches of rain fell, causing loss of both life and property. CERT volunteers assisted in a number of support activities, including:

- Directing traffic
- Filling sandbags
- Delivering supplies to elderly residents and emergency responders
- Staffing city phones
- Documenting damage
- Relaying important safety information to residents
- Maintaining security around affected areas

Olympic Trials - Eugene, Oregon - June 2008
The U.S. Olympic Track and Field Trials in Eugene, Oregon, attracted daily crowds of more than 25,000 people. CERTs were initially activated to assist the Eugene Fire Department. Due to a volunteer shortage, their role was expanded. They performed duties such as:

- Checking bags and wanding attendees
- Helping with crowd control
- Assisting with traffic control
- Providing directions to citizens
- Helping lost individuals
- Assisting those with special needs

Power Outage - Miami, Florida - June 2008
During a recent regional and statewide power outage in Miami, Florida, the University of Miami 'Canes Community Emergency Response Team was activated. The team assisted with traffic management at congested intersections where traffic signals were out. The local police station had previously trained many University of Miami CERT members in traffic management. They assisted professionals with their quick, coordinated response and excellent skills.

Why Do Communities Need CERTs?

Disasters can put lives and property in your community at risk while overwhelming resources. Widespread damage may create more needs than can be immediately met. If communication, medical, or transportation systems suffer serious damage, responder action can be delayed.

What kind of damage do you think can prevent a quick response?

Infrastructure Damage and Response

Damage to the infrastructure restricts the ability of first-response personnel to identify and respond to those in need. Significant damage to the infrastructure includes:

- Transportation
    - Inability to assess damage accurately
    - Ambulances prevented from reaching survivors
    - Police prevented from reaching damaged areas
    - Fire department prevented from reaching fires
    - Flow of needed supplies interrupted
- Structures
    - Damaged hospitals unable to function normally
    - Increased risk of injury from falling debris
- Communication Systems
    - Survivors unable to call for help
    - Coordination of services hampered
- Utilities
    - Loss of utilities
    - Increased risk of fire resulting from gas or electrical problems
    - Inadequate water supply
    - Increased risk to public health
- Water Service
    - Firefighting capabilities restricted
    - Medical facilities hampered
- Fuel Supplies
    - Increased risk of fire or explosion from fuel line ruptures
    - Risk of asphyxiation
    - Flow of needed supplies interrupted

CERT Training and Safety

When a community suffers damage caused by a natural or manmade disaster, CERT members have the chance to be of great assistance to neighbors, co-workers, and others. But remember: CERT members are not trained or equipped to handle incidents as professional responders. And CERT members are trained to always keep themselves safe while helping others.

CERTs Augment Response Resources

The multiple effects of a disaster can put a strain on local and surrounding resources. And when their resources are taxed, emergency services must focus on the highest-priority needs. For example:

1. Police address incidents having a **grave** impact on public safety.
2. Firefighters suppress **major** fires.
3. EMS personnel focus on **mass** casualty events they can reach.

Emergency services will take time to respond to these and other needs. This is where CERTs come in.

As a CERT member, you can provide valuable assistance by addressing the needs that may arise before professional responders can arrive in your neighborhood or workplace.

Do you want to learn how actual CERT members feel about their role in the community?

CERTs Make a Difference

You will now have an opportunity to see how CERT members make a difference in their communities.

Allen Abbott
It's a fantastic program. I think it should be taught in every community across the country, and, if it was, then the response that the professional community has to give would be reduced, and even the little day-to-day emergencies would be minimized for the general public, if everybody took it. I'm part of the solution and not adding to the problem, probably most important.

Jamie Garvelle
I've been a volunteer in a lot of different areas, and this was just one more place to get some knowledge and experience and hopefully be of assistance. It's kind of a mindset. The people who come out and do this have a tendency to be people who care about the community anyway, so you've got that in common from the start.

John Clark
CERT is important because it provides hands-on training and an awareness of what's going on in your community. That also gives you resources to call upon yourself in order to take care of your family, and it's kind of like an expanding ripple, kind of like dropping a rock in a pond and the ripple out for a CERT person. Our goal is to make sure we are safe and protected. Then we move out to the next level and check our family, and from there we move out to our community and make sure our neighborhood is safe and that everyone is taken care of, and from there we move out to our actual CERT staging area. So it's a multi-part program and concept that we use to make sure our community and our neighborhoods are safe and protected.

Sara Trimble
We had an earthquake here a couple of years ago, and it definitely shook everybody up, and you realize once again why you're doing this, you know, if something happened, I want to feel like I have something to contribute to help and not feel like I'm stuck, not knowing what to do. CERT certainly gives you a

background in what you can do to be helpful and what you shouldn't do, too, you know, that might get yourself in trouble.

Knowledge Review

Review each statement and then indicate if it is true or false.

1.　T　F　CERTs operating in their neighborhoods can extend the capabilities of response organizations.

2.　T　F　CERT requires volunteers to be extensively trained so that they can take the place of emergency responders.

3.　T　F　When response resources are limited, emergency services usually convert to a first-come, first-served basis for deploying personnel.

4.　T　F　Damage to the infrastructure often restricts the capabilities of response services.

Answers:
　　1. T
　　2. F
　　3. F
　　4. T

The Role of CERTs

Now, let's look at CERT roles. Effective CERTs are well-organized, well-trained, and well-managed.

Two common roles you will have as a CERT member are in hazard mitigation and disaster response. You will learn more about these in Lesson 1-2, but let's discuss them briefly now.

Safety

Remember: In all CERT activities, your safety is the number one priority!

Hazard Mitigation and CERTs

Hazard mitigation involves taking preventive actions both before and after a disaster.

First, you reduce hazards in the home or workplace **before** a disaster occurs. Then, you act immediately **after** an event to minimize damage and risk.

Examples of CERT mitigation activities include:

- Eliminating unnecessary hazardous materials from your home
- Ensuring that none of your electrical outlets are overloaded
- Shutting off gas meters that are leaking after an event

Now let's discuss disaster response.

Disaster Response and CERTs

Based on your local CERT Program's operating procedures, you may respond in your area following a disaster. CERT members are trained to provide help when professional responders are delayed. And once professional responders arrive, you may be asked to assist them with critical support activities.

CERT training is critical to your response. A few examples of the training you will receive are:

- Locating and turning off utilities when it is safe to do so
- Extinguishing small fires safely
- Treating life-threatening injuries until professional assistance can be obtained
- Conducting light search and rescue operations
- Helping survivors cope with trauma

You'll learn more about these response activities in later lessons, which will prepare you for the hands-on *CERT Basic Training* course in the classroom.

Non-disaster CERT Roles

CERT members can be valuable resources in their communities by helping with community events and public safety projects. CERT members:

- May go into a community before a disaster to identify and aid community members who may need help during a disaster. One way they can help is to verify and update a list of special needs residents who have previously registered with local emergency responders. This list enables local emergency personnel, who carry a copy of the list with them, to know who is a priority during an event. The CERT will verify the address and needs of each person on the list. While doing so, the team can also give a list of items the person should take when he or she evacuates, and conduct a basic safety check of the home and smoke detectors.

- Can distribute preparedness materials and conduct preparedness demonstrations. They may speak to current CERT classes undergoing training, or be asked to speak at community centers or homeowners associations. They can explain the purpose of CERT and hand out helpful information on being prepared for a disaster. They may also hand out materials on behalf of local emergency management personnel, ensuring that their community has the most up-to-date information to prepare for an event.
- Staff parades, health fairs, county fairs, and other special events. This enables CERT members to provide helpful information to their community. This could be an informational pamphlet about CERT or something distributed on behalf of local emergency management personnel. Or it could be CERT members staffing the first aid or lost child areas at a county fair. A CERT in Los Angeles frequently staffs the finish line of the LA Marathon. The team hands out water, administers basic first aid, and brings runners to the medical tent.
- Can assist with the installation of smoke alarms for seniors and special needs households. Members receive training on how to install smoke detectors and answer basic fire and life safety questions. Some areas also have smoke detector hotlines. Residents phone in their questions and hotline staff contact a nearby CERT member to assist residents with their needs.
- May provide parade route traffic management and traffic and crowd control at other events. Members can assist by covering intersections and other areas not being covered by police. In the case of parades, CERT members work to guide traffic and pedestrians out of the path of the parade. At other events, such as a marathon, members keep runners on the correct route and pedestrians from being where they shouldn't be.

Knowledge Review

1.   T   F   Reducing potential fire hazards in your home is an example of a hazard mitigation action.

2.   T   F   The CERT member's role is to promote disaster preparedness; CERT members very rarely become involved in disaster response.

3.   T   F   As a CERT member, your number one priority is to ensure the safety of those in need.

4.   T   F   Part of your CERT training will include learning how to extinguish small fires and how to conduct light search and rescue operations.

Answers:
1. T
2. F
3. F
4. T

Lesson Summary

In this lesson, you learned that:

- Disasters may overwhelm emergency response resources.
- CERTs can extend the capabilities of response organizations through hazard mitigation and response activities.
- Before a disaster, CERTs focus on emergency preparedness and hazard mitigation.
- After a disaster, CERTs may operate directly or assist responders in activities to save or sustain lives and protect property.

You have completed this lesson. You are now ready to begin Lesson 1-2: Family and Workplace Preparedness.

Module 1: CERT Basics
Lesson 1-2: Family and Workplace Preparedness

Lesson Overview

Welcome to Lesson 1-2: Family and Workplace Preparedness.

As a CERT member, you may have opportunities to help with preparing your neighborhood or workplace for a disaster. This lesson teaches you preparedness strategies that you can use at home or work.

After completing this lesson, you should be able to:

- Identify hazard mitigation strategies
- Identify the steps for developing a family disaster plan
- Select the necessary items to include in disaster supply kits

It should take you approximately **35 minutes** to complete this lesson.

Overview

CERTs support emergency services by preparing for disasters before they occur. Once you become a trained CERT member, you can respond, when necessary, to immediate needs in your neighborhood or workplace after a disaster occurs. But first, you need to be sure that you're prepared at home and at work.

Are You Ready?

Think about your home and workplace. Are you prepared for a disaster?

Preparedness

Preparedness is the key to protecting lives and property when a disaster strikes. This means taking steps before a disaster occurs to lessen the impact so you're prepared to take action when needed.

Before You Begin

Remember that, as a CERT member, your first responsibility is to ensure that your family and neighbors are safe.

A good place to start is with the FEMA publication, *Are You Ready? An In-depth Guide to Citizen Preparedness.* You may want to review this document before continuing with this lesson.

You can access *Are You Ready?* at the following web address: http://www.ready.gov/are-you-ready-guide.

Another source for preparedness information is the *Ready* site. It includes general information as well as material for specific groups, such as older individuals, military families, people with disabilities, and pet owners. You can access *Ready* materials at http://www.ready.gov.

Home and Workplace Preparedness

There are two important areas to address as you prepare your home and workplace: hazard mitigation and disaster preparations.

In hazard mitigation, identify potential hazards in your home and workplace. Then take the appropriate steps to remove or reduce them.

In disaster preparations, make plans and preparations that will enable you to respond quickly in the event of a disaster.

Hazard Mitigation

There are three steps to hazard mitigation:

1. Determining your community's probable disaster threats
2. Identifying potential hazards in your home and workplace
3. Taking preventive action to reduce the hazards

Mitigation Step 1: Determine Disaster Threats

The first step is to know which disasters are likely to affect your community. Some common disaster threats are:

- Earthquake
- Flood

- Winter storm
- Fire
- Hurricane
- Tornado
- Landslide/debris flow
- Wildfire
- Tsunami
- Hazardous materials
- Volcanic eruption
- Heat wave
- Nuclear incident
- Terrorism

Once you know the threats, you can identify potential hazards, such as ...

Threats and Hazards

These are a few examples of hazards based on threat:
- Wildfire: Flammable roofing materials and brush and vegetation
- Earthquake: Unsecured objects, such as a bookshelf or filing cabinet
- Flood: Utilities below flood level

Determining Disaster Threats: Questions to Ask

Disaster threats can be:

- Natural
- Technological
- Adversarial or Human Caused

To identify probable events in your community and their likely impacts, there are several questions you can ask yourself. Let's see what a current CERT member asks himself.

Questions to Ask

This CERT member asks himself the following questions:

- Am I in a floodplain, near a fault, or near a volcano?
- Is my region prone to seasonal hazards, such as hurricanes, tornadoes, or winter storms?

- Are nearby sites likely terrorism targets?
- Am I near a nuclear or chemical plant that could release hazardous materials?

Can you think of any other important questions to ask as you identify probable events and impacts in your community?

Knowledge Review

What types of disasters might be most likely to affect your community? Write your answers below and compare to the answers given.

____
____
____
____
____

Answers:
A community might be at risk for any of the following events:
- Earthquake
- Flood
- Winter storm
- Fire
- Hurricane
- Tornado
- Landslide/debris flow
- Wildfire
- Volcanic eruptions
- Tsunami
- Heat wave
- Hazardous materials (chemical emergency)
- Terrorism
- Nuclear incident

Possible sources you can contact for additional information about your particular community include:
- Local emergency manager
- Fire department
- Local librarian
- Local chapter of the American Red Cross
- State department of natural resources

The more you know, the better you will be able to plan, prepare, and take preventive action. For more information about disaster threats, visit:
http://www.ready.gov/are-you-ready-guide

Mitigation Step 2: Identify Hazards

The second step in hazard mitigation is to identify hazards. A good place to start is with buildings. Buildings that are harmless most of the time often have features that can become dangerous during a storm. Identify hazards based on two main groups:

- Structural: hazards that are a function of the building, roof, or other components
- Nonstructural: hazards related to fixtures and building contents

Let's talk about structural hazards first.

Structural Hazards

Types of structural hazards and their significance vary according to the:

- Age of the structure
- Type of construction
- Type of disaster

Here are four examples of common structural hazards.

- Home Not Bolted to Foundation
    - Homes built before 1940 generally were not bolted to the foundation. They are subject to being shaken, blown, or floated off their foundations.
- Unreinforced Brick Construction
    - Older homes constructed of unreinforced masonry are less stable than a new construction.
- Mobile Home
    - Mobile homes are easily displaced. Displacement can destroy structural integrity and break gas and electric lines, increasing the risk of fire and electric shock.
- Long Roof Span
    - Buildings with long roof spans are subject to roof collapse.

Knowledge Review

What are some potential structural hazards in your home? Write your answers
below and compare to the answers given.

____

____

____

____

____

Answer:

Typical structural hazards:

- House not bolted to the foundation (earthquake, flood, tornado)
- Mobile home not strapped to the slab (earthquake, flood, landslide, tornado)
- Loose fuel tank (earthquake, flood, landslide, tornado)
- Utilities below flood level (flood)
- Rigid gas piping that could pull away from a moved appliance (earthquake, flood, landslide)
- Deep cracks or loose materials in the foundation, ceilings, roof, or chimney (earthquake, hurricane, tornado)
- Long roof expanses (earthquake, hurricane, tornado, winter storm)
- Large expanses of glass (earthquake, hurricane, tornado, winter storm)
- Panels that could fall (earthquake, hurricane, tornado)

If you are concerned about structural integrity, you may need to consult with
experts, such as structural engineers, architects, or soil engineers. FEMA also
provides information about reducing structural hazards in its online library: _
http://www.fema.gov/resource-document-library

Nonstructural Hazards

The second type of hazard is nonstructural. These hazards can occur in any
structure and are items installed after the supporting structure of the building is
complete. These may be hazards in their own right or become hazards after an
event.

You should consider utility fixtures and building contents as nonstructural hazards.

Utility Fixtures

Gas, electric, and water lines can create a hazard for your family or neighbors. You
should be aware of utility fixtures that could create a problem at your home or
workplace. These are just a few examples of the problems utilities may create:

- Broken gas line connections from water heaters or ranges displaced by shaking, water, or wind
- Electric shock hazards from displaced appliances and office equipment
- Fire hazards from faulty wiring, overloaded electrical sockets or extension cords, and frayed electrical cords
- Utility boxes and electrical outlets below flood level in flood zones

Unsecured Building Contents

You should also consider unsecured building contents when you identify nonstructural hazards. Loose contents can cause damage or hurt someone when they fall. You should be especially aware of this hazard if your area is prone to earthquakes. Here are a few examples that you should look for:

- Unsecured furniture, appliances, and heavy objects on tables
- Items on open shelves
- Mirrors and pictures on walls — especially when above a sofa or bed
- Breakable items or chemicals stored in unfastened cabinets

Knowledge Review

What are some potential nonstructural hazards in your home and workplace? Write your answers below and compare to the answers given.

____
____
____
____
____

Answers:
Typical nonstructural hazards:
- Hot water heater that could move (earthquake, flood)
- Bookshelf or filing cabinet that could overturn (earthquake, flood, tornado)
- Picture or heavy mirror that could fall off the wall onto a couch or bed (earthquake)
- Appliances and office equipment that could fall (earthquake, flood)
- Unbraced overhead lighting fixture (earthquake)
- Breakable items, such as dishes, stored in cupboards without latches (earthquake)
- Electrical hazards (e.g., overloaded circuits)

- Chemical and fire hazards (e.g., flammable liquids stored on open shelves) (earthquake, flood, hurricane, landslide)
- Lack of smoke alarms or sprinkler systems

To obtain additional information, conduct a room-by-room walk-through. Keep in mind the types of disasters that pose a probable threat in your community. FEMA also provides information about reducing nonstructural hazards in its online library: http://www.fema.gov/resource-document-library

Mitigation Step 3: Take Preventive Action

The final step in hazard mitigation is to take preventive action. After you've determined likely threats and identified potential hazards in your home or workplace, it's time to correct or reduce any hazards.

Mitigating Structural Hazards

There are several things you can do to reduce your risk of a structural hazard. A few examples include:

- Bolting older house to the foundation
- Strapping mobile home to the slab
- Raising utilities above the level of flood risk
- Repairing an unstable chimney, roof, and foundation

Mitigating Nonstructural Hazards

You can reduce your risk of nonstructural hazards as well. A few examples include:
- Anchoring furniture such as bookshelves, filing cabinets, and hutches to the wall
- Strapping a water heater to wall studs
- Installing flexible pipe fittings to avoid gas or water leaks
- Securing office equipment in place with industrial-strength Velcro®
- Securing cabinet doors with childproof fasteners
- Moving heavy objects to lower shelves and cabinets
- Replacing picture hangers with earthquake-resistant hooks
- Securing propane tanks

Knowledge Review

What are some potential mitigation actions that you can take to make your home or workplace safer? Write your answers below and compare to the answers given.

____
____
____
____
____

Answer:
There are many possible answers, depending on the particulars of your home and your location.

Compare your answers to the suggestions provided in the *Are You Ready?* document:
- Part 2: Natural Hazards
    - Section 1
    - Section 2
- Part 3: Technological Hazards
- Part 4: Terrorism

Family Preparedness

Hazard mitigation is just the first part of protecting your home and workplace. Preparedness also includes making plans that will enable you and your family to respond quickly in the event of a disaster. You should develop a comprehensive plan for how your family will respond to various hazards.

How prepared is your family for a disaster? Complete the emergency planning checklist here. (You can complete one for your workplace, too.)

Checklist for Home Preparedness

Plan	YES	NO
Develop an escape plan that covers every room in the house and considers the needs of children and physically challenged individuals.		
Pick two places to meet (near home and outside the neighborhood).		
Choose an out-of-state "check-in contact" for everyone to call.		
Identify an evacuation destination.		
Plan two evacuation routes (in case your primary route is impassable).		
Identify the nearest shelter location.		
Plan how to take care of your pets (generally not allowed in shelters).		
Find safe places in the home for each type of disaster.		
Make sure that you have adequate insurance coverage.		
Inventory your property to help prove the value of items damaged or destroyed in a disaster.		
Review your plan periodically and update, if necessary.		
Practice	**YES**	**NO**
Discuss the plan with all family members.		
Conduct family practices (fire drills, taking shelter, following evacuation routes).		
Make sure that family members know where fire extinguishers are and how to use them.		
Show responsible family members how and when to shut off water, gas, and electricity at main switches.		
Quiz children every six months to be sure that they remember the plan.		
Prepare	**YES**	**NO**
Post emergency numbers by every phone.		
Locate and label utility shutoffs.		
Install smoke alarms on every level (especially near bedrooms).		

Test smoke alarms monthly, change batteries twice a year.		
Check fire extinguishers according to manufacturer's instructions.		
Prepare a safe room for sheltering in place.		
Photocopy vital documents. Keep originals in a safe deposit box, store one copy at home, and give a copy to someone out of town.		
Assemble a disaster supply kit.		
Coordinate with Neighbors	**YES**	**NO**
Plan how neighbors can work together after a disaster.		
Identify neighbors' skills (e.g., medical or technical).		
Identify neighbors with special needs (e.g., elderly, disabled) who may need help in an emergency.		
Make plans for child care in case parents can't get home.		

Disaster Supply Kit

It's important to be prepared. Assembling the supplies that you might need following a disaster is an important part of your family disaster plan. A disaster supply kit should include:

- Basic disaster supplies
- Evacuation supplies stored in an easy-to-carry container
- Home disaster supplies for sheltering in place

You can complete your own disaster supply kit checklist to see how ready you are.

Disaster Supply Kit Checklist

Basic Kit	YES	NO
Portable, battery-powered radio or TV and extra batteries		
Flashlight and extra batteries		
First aid kit and first aid manual		
Supply of prescription medications or copies of prescriptions		
Credit card and cash		
Personal identification and important family documents (insurance policies, identification, bank account records, all kept in a waterproof, portable container)		
An extra set of keys		
Matches in a waterproof container		
Signal flare		
Special items (e.g., diapers or formula, hearing aid batteries, spare wheelchair battery, spare eyeglasses, or other items for physical needs.)		
Evacuation Supplies: Basic kit plus the following items, packed in a portable carrier (e.g., duffle bag), labeled, and stored in a convenient location.	**YES**	**NO**
Plan to have one gallon of water per person per day, for three days, for drinking and sanitation. Children, nursing mothers, and sick people may need more water. If you live in a warm-weather climate, more water may be necessary. Store water tightly in clean plastic containers, such as soft drink bottles. Don't use plastic milk jugs to store water.		
Store at least a 3-day supply of non-perishable food. Select foods that require no refrigeration, preparation, or cooking and little or no water. (Protein or fruit bars, dry cereal or granola, peanut butter, dried fruit, nuts, crackers, canned juices, non-perishable pasteurized milk, high-energy foods, vitamins, infant food, comfort/stress food, and canned meats, fruits, and vegetables)		

Item		
Kitchen accessories (can opener, utensils, utility knife, cooking fuel, bleach to treat drinking water, sugar, salt, pepper, plastic bags, aluminum foil)		
Change of clothing and footwear		
Weather protection (gloves, jacket, raincoat, sunscreen, hat, etc.)		
Sanitation/hygiene items (toothbrush, toothpaste, soap, comb, toilet paper, plastic bags, tissues, sanitary napkins, moist towelettes)		
Local map marked with evacuation routes		
Communication kit (contact numbers, cell phone or coins for pay phone)		
Blankets or sleeping bags		
Tools and other items (paper and pencil, needles and thread, pliers, shutoff wrench, shovels, tape, medicine dropper, whistle, plastic sheeting, fire extinguisher, emergency preparedness manual, tube tent, compass)		
Entertainment (e.g., books and games)		
Home Disaster Supplies: Basic kit and evacuation kit plus the following items	**YES**	**NO**
Additional blankets and sleeping bags		
Wrench to turn off utilities (stored near shutoff valves)		
If you live in a cold-weather climate, think about warmth. It's possible the power will be out and you will not have heat. Have at least one complete change of warm clothing and shoes per person, including: a jacket or coat, long pants, long sleeve shirt, sturdy shoes, and a hat and gloves.		

Knowledge Review

You're packing a disaster supply kit. There are a few important items that you need to add. Select all the items from the list below that you should add to a disaster supply kit.

A. Toothbrush
B. Can opener
C. First aid kit
D. Dress shoes
E. Wrench
F. Notepad and pencil
G. Cell phone
H. Chainsaw
I. Laptop computer
J. Cash and credit cards
K. Golf clubs
L. Blender

Answer:
A, B, C, E, F, G, J

Stay or Go?

If there's a chance for a disaster, how do I know if I should stay or go?

Evacuation vs. Sheltering in Place

Even if you've done everything right to prepare at home or in the office, the situation still may require you to evacuate. Should you evacuate or shelter in place? If you're near an incident site, evaluate the situation and determine what to do. The decision is not always easy.

If your time and location allow, listen to the Emergency Alert System (EAS). Emergency management professionals who are evaluating the incident may provide instructions and tips.

Either way, there are precautions you can take.

Evacuation

If you choose evacuation, or if emergency managers require evacuation, be sure to take steps to ensure your safety. For instance, always keep your evacuation supplies in a convenient location. Some people keep their supplies in the car trunk.

And if you do own a car, keep your gas tank full or nearly full — especially during high-risk months for seasonal hazards. If you don't own a car, make alternate arrangements for transportation with friends or local government.

Remember: If you have children, know their school's procedures for an evacuation.

Sheltering in Place

Depending on your situation, staying inside may be safer than evacuating. If this is the case, know what to do for the specific hazards in your area.

You should select a safe room ahead of time, preferably an interior room with no (or few) windows. Have your disaster supply kit ready, as well as water, food, and snacks. Books and other supplies can make the situation more comfortable. And remember to have food for your pets!

Stay tuned to the Emergency Alert System (EAS) for additional instructions. You should also be aware of local and national warning systems and where to get information as a disaster progresses (e.g., NOAA Weather Radio).

You will learn more about sheltering in place during the classroom *CERT Basic Training* course.

Knowledge Review

Which of the following are procedures for sheltering in place?

    A. Move to an interior room
    B. Listen to a local or national warning system
    C. Have water, food, and snacks available
    D. Create a sheltering-in-place disaster kit

Answer:
A, B, C

Lesson Summary

Before a disaster strikes, you should:

- Identify potential hazards in the home and workplace
- Take steps to mitigate those hazards
- Develop and practice a family disaster plan
- Assemble a disaster supply kit

You have completed this lesson. You are now ready to begin Lesson 1-3: CERT Organization.

Module 1: CERT Basics
Lesson 1-3: CERT Organization

Lesson Overview

Welcome to Lesson 1-3: CERT Organization.

Effective team organization is vital to fulfilling the CERT goal of augmenting response resources. Good organization allows protocol to be followed and ensures the safety of team members. This lesson explains how CERTs are organized and how they tie into overall incident response. You will learn more about team organization during the classroom training.

After completing this lesson, you should be able to:

*   State the role of the Incident Command System (ICS) in CERT organization
*   Explain how CERT decision-making relates to rescuer safety

It should take you approximately **25 minutes** to complete this lesson.

Basics for CERT Participation

The first part of an organized CERT program is an Emergency Operations Plan (EOP). This plan is developed by your local professional response agencies and describes how your community will prepare for, respond to, and recover from an emergency or disaster.

CERTs are part of the response organization outlined in the EOP. At all times, CERTs operate according to policies established by the local emergency response agency.

What can be found in an EOP?

Elements of an EOP

EOP:

*   Establishes emergency management and emergency response organization using the Incident Command System (ICS) and assigns responsibility for key positions
*   Establishes lines of authority and coordination among government departments and agencies, and community organizations

- Describes how protection will be provided for people and property
- Identifies available response resources

Where Will You Fit?

You will now have an opportunity to learn what three CERT members have to say about how they fit into their CERT organization.

You will have the chance to perform a number of different jobs as a CERT member. CERT offers opportunities for you to build on skills you already have or find something completely new to contribute to your team. Let's see what three CERT members have to say about how they fit into their CERT organization.

Sandy Bastille
A sudden thunderstorm in our community brought high winds, along with bigger than usual waves that washed over the shore causing flooding on our streets and sidewalks. The water pouring onto the streets and sidewalks was just phenomenal. People were scurrying around trying to get out of the way of the water. The first responders responded quickly, then CERT members were activated and they stepped right in. They proactively coordinated the people in the streets, ensuring that everyone in the community was accounted for and safe. The first responders set up barricades and CERTs were asked to direct everyone away from the flooding to higher ground since those areas weren't inundated with water. The public works department set about their work and, because of the safety zones that were set up around the barricades, they were able to move their equipment safely without fear of anyone being in their way. The barricades allowed us to quickly identify what the actual danger spots were and make sure that people kept clear of those areas.

Sara Trimble
I've gotten into the disaster programs within the hospitals, both the one I work at and the one that's close by, and helping their disaster committees come up with plans, what to do should there be disasters, as well as providing communications support via the ham frequencies.

John Clark
There are multiple roles in CERT, and in our group we've all kind of gravitated to our specialty. I'm an outdoor person, so I like to be outdoors. I kind of gravitate more toward the urban search and rescue, being out in the front line, checking things out and providing information back to our CERT director.

The Incident Command System

To understand the CERT organization, it is helpful to know a little about the Incident Command System (ICS).

Professional responders use ICS to manage and respond to emergencies and disasters. CERT uses ICS for the same reason.

The basic ICS structure is established by the first person at the scene, who becomes the Incident Commander (IC).

ICS Expansion

In a small incident, the IC may handle all duties — much like a police officer at a traffic accident. In larger events, the IC delegates responsibility for some duties to make the overall response more manageable.

The ICS structure is designed to be flexible, expanding and contracting with the needs of the incident. As needs and demands at the incident expand, the IC will assign people, called Section Chiefs, to help manage the incident. As the incident expands further, tasks that need to be accomplished are assigned to one of the ICS Sections.

ICS Chart

Each ICS job comes with its own duties, as seen below:

Incident Commander:

- Leader
- Decides what is to be done

Operations Section Chief:

- Doer
- Implements the decisions made by the IC

Logistics Section Chief:

- Getter
- Ensures that the personnel, equipment, and tools required by operations to implement the IC's decisions are in the right place, at the right time, in the right quantities

Planning Section Chief:

- Thinker
- Receives, filters, and compiles information coming in from incident scene

Administration Section Chief:

- Recorder
- Collects all incident data after they have been compiled, acted on, and/or are no longer needed.

CERT Organization in a Disaster

The government agency that sponsors your local CERT Program will establish local protocols for CERT activation and operations. These local protocols will be based on ICS and, when working in their neighborhood or workplace, team members will use ICS to manage CERT activities.

As a CERT member, you first respond to a disaster by reporting to your neighborhood or workplace staging area with your supplies. Along the way, record the locations and types of damage you see. You'll use this information to establish priorities and make decisions about if and how the team will respond.

The CERT Team Leader

The first CERT member to arrive becomes the Incident Commander (IC). The IC will begin managing operations until the designated CERT Team Leader arrives.

Once the Team Leader arrives at the staging area, he or she will assume the responsibilities for managing CERT operations. Let's say you are the Team Leader. What are your duties?

- First, make your ICS position assignments. Prioritize the CERT response to the incident so that you can do the most good for the most people.
- Then you should ensure that information is continually gathered about injuries and damage. Make sure you document these findings and all other team operations.
- And don't forget to communicate and coordinate with professional responders. You will continue to manage operations until you are relieved by a professional responder on the scene.

CERT Teams

CERT members may operate as a single team that performs all activities as required. But CERT members may also be assigned to smaller teams. Teams will be assigned based on incident needs. Typical team assignments include:

- Fire Suppression Teams
- Search and Rescue Teams
- Medical Teams

Team Makeup

If the incident does call for smaller teams, each team must have at least three members and a designated leader.

The designated Team Leader is responsible for ensuring team safety, communicating with the Section Chief, and carrying out the assigned tasks. Two team members become a "buddy team" and respond to incidents as directed. The other member serves as a runner and relays messages between the team and the Operations Section Chief at the Incident Command Post (ICP).

The Incident Command Post

The CERT Incident Command Post (ICP) is set up near the staging area. From this location, the CERT Team Leader and Section Chiefs manage and direct CERT activities.

If you, as Team Leader, have to leave the ICP for any reason, you should pass the responsibility for team operations to another CERT member. This person will then become the Incident Commander.

Benefits of the CERT Structure

An organizational structure helps CERT leaders and members to be more effective and focused in their response. An accountability system and management structure helps ensure the safety of the team. Organization also makes communication, information management, and activity documentation more effective.

The result of a structured approach is what matters the most: the ability to direct team responses to do the most good for the most people.

Remember, the government agency that sponsors your local CERT Program establishes other important protocols that all local CERTs must follow. You'll learn about these protocols in the classroom *CERT Basic Training* course.

CERT Mobilization

When an incident occurs, you should first take care of matters close to home. This includes handling any concerns related to:

* Yourself
* Your family
* Your home
* Your immediate neighbors
* Your CERT

You will not be able to function effectively as a CERT member before handling these concerns. Once you have resolved matters in your immediate area, you should function according to your team's Standard Operating Procedures.

Communication

Two-way communication between the CERT Team Leader and CERT teams operating in the field is vital.

Situations and priorities may change rapidly during a response. The CERT Team Leader must be aware of these changes and communicate changing information to members in the field. Doing so helps to ensure that CERT members act safely and do the greatest good for the greatest number.

Two-way communication also plays an important role in decision-making.

CERT Decision-Making

Good decisions depend on reliable and current information. An open line of communication between the CERT Team Leader and the CERTs and individual CERT members in the field ensures that they all have the most recent information about disaster events. This information then allows CERTs to make decisions and tailor their response to the changing situation efficiently and safely.

And because team safety is always the first priority, **all** decisions will be made with one key question in mind ...

Is It Safe?

Is it safe for me to attempt this task?

CERT Documentation

Mobilization and decision-making also require documentation. You can play a role in incident documentation and maintain an efficient flow of information for your team. Documentation has many uses. It's a good way to account for team members and deploy them where they will do the most good. Once on the scene, they can document damages and track injuries.

Putting the situation in print can also help you develop an understanding of the overall situation. This can be especially helpful when professional responders arrive on the scene. Be prepared to provide them with your assembled documentation as soon as they arrive.

Standard forms are available for many types of CERT documentation. You will learn more about documentation and using the forms in the CERT classroom training.

Knowledge Review

What is most critical to CERT decision-making?

        A. Ongoing communication
        B. Team assignments
        C. Training in ICS
        D. Taking care of your neighbors

Answer:
A

Lesson Summary

In this lesson, you learned that:

- The ICS is used to manage emergency operations.
- CERTs use ICS, which expands and contracts as needed to handle the situation.
- Efficient two-way communication is essential for effective decision-making.
- The CERT decision-making process is guided by the goal of CERT safety.

Now, let's review what you learned in this module and then see what you can expect to learn about in the next module.

Module Summary

In Module 1: CERT Basics, you learned that:

- Disasters may overwhelm emergency response resources.
- CERTs can extend the capabilities of response organizations through hazard mitigation and response activities.
- Before a disaster, CERTs focus on emergency preparedness and hazard mitigation.
- After a disaster, CERTs may operate directly or assist responders in activities to save or sustain lives and protect property.
- There are many types of potential hazards in the home and workplace and ways to mitigate those hazards.
- You should develop and practice a family disaster plan.
- A disaster supply kit includes basic items that members of a household will need in the event of a disaster.
- The ICS is used to manage emergency operations.
- CERTs use ICS, which expands and contracts as needed to handle the situation.
- Efficient two-way communication is essential for effective decision-making.
- The CERT decision-making process is guided by the goal of CERT safety.

What's Next

Now it's time to move on to Module 2: Fire Safety. You'll learn things such as the role of CERTs in fire safety, how to identify potential fire hazards in your home, how to mitigate those hazards, and the importance of safe practices for fire suppression.

Module 2: Fire Safety
Lesson 2-1: Introduction to Fire Safety

Module Overview

Welcome to Module 2: Fire Safety.

Fires are frequently among the hazards encountered when disaster strikes. Professional firefighters focus on saving lives and putting out major fires, while often contending with obstacles beyond their control, such as impassable roads and violent weather.

As a CERT member, there's a lot you can do to help with fire safety. Some actions that you can take, such as helping with evacuations, directly assist professional firefighters during a disaster. Other actions you can take are equally useful at disaster sites, in your own home, and at your workplace. These include steps such as:

- Recognizing and correcting fire hazards
- Shutting off utilities when necessary to prevent fires
- Putting out small fires

In this module, you'll learn about practices for mitigating fire hazards and the procedures involved in safely putting out small fires.

It should take about **1½ hours** to complete the three lessons in this module:

- Lesson 2-1: Introduction to Fire Safety — **35 minutes**
- Lesson 2-2: Fire Hazards in the Home and Workplace — **30 minutes**
- Lesson 2-3: Safe Fire Suppression — **25 minutes**

After completing this module, you should be able to:

Identify fire safety practices that CERTs must follow

Lesson Overview

Welcome to Lesson 2-1: Introduction to Fire Safety.

In this lesson you'll learn about the role of CERTs in fire safety, the basic principles of fire chemistry, and the different firefighting resources that are available for fighting different classes of fires.

The other lessons in Module 2 will build on this foundation. A good understanding of these fire safety fundamentals is also essential before you take the classroom-based *CERT Basic Training* course in fire safety.

After completing this lesson, you should be able to:

- State the role of CERTs in fire safety
- Correlate fire classification with firefighting resources

It should take you about **35 minutes** to complete this lesson.

Fire Chemistry

What does it take for a fire to burn? Three elements:

- **Fuel**, or material to be burned, which may be a liquid, a solid, or a gas
- **Heat** that raises the temperature of the fuel to its ignition point
- And **oxygen** – Without an atmosphere of at least 20 percent oxygen, most fuels can be heated until they entirely vaporize, without burning.

Together, fuel, heat, and oxygen — called the fire triangle — create a chemical exothermic reaction, or, simply put, fire.

If you take any one of these elements away and permanently interrupt the reaction, the fire goes out. This concept is the basis for fire suppression, as we'll discuss later.

Which one of the three elements do you think is especially important when you have to make decisions about how to extinguish a fire?

exothermic reaction: *A reaction in which heat is given off*

Fuel is especially important when you have to make decisions about how to extinguish a fire. Why? Because the type and amount of fuel determines the fire classification, and that, in turn, tells you which equipment and methods to use to put the fire out.

To explain this, let's begin with how fires are classified.

There are five classes of fire: A, B, C, D, and ...?

Fire Classification

... K is the fifth class of fire. Each class of fire is fed by different types of fuel, as shown in the table below.

Fire	Fuel	Notes
Class A	Ordinary combustibles, such as: • Paper • Wood • Cloth • Rubber	These fuels leave ash after they burn up.
Class B	• Flammable liquids, such as oil and gasoline • Combustible liquids, such as charcoal lighter fluid and kerosene	These fuels burn only at the surface because oxygen can't penetrate the depth of the fluid. Only the vapor burns when ignited.
Class C	Electrical equipment, such as wiring and motors	When the electricity is turned off and is no longer feeding the fire, the fire becomes a Class A or B fire, depending on the type of fuel.
Class D	Combustible metals, such as • Aluminum • Titanium • Zirconium • Magnesium • Potassium	Class D fires are not normally found in residential areas.
Class K	• Cooking oils (vegetable or animal) • Fats used in cooking appliances	Class K fires are technically flammable liquid/gas fires (Class B), but because of their special characteristics, they are placed in a separate class. Class K can occur in commercial food preparation locations, such as restaurant kitchens, where large quantities of cooking oils are used.

Knowledge Review

During an extremely hot day, gasoline-soaked rags in an unventilated shed catch fire. What classification of fire is this?

    A. Class A
    B. Class B
    C. Class C
    D. Class D
    E. Class K

Answer:
B

Knowledge Review

Accumulated residue of cooking oil ignites in the hood above the commercial range in a restaurant. What classification of fire is this?

    A. Class A
    B. Class B
    C. Class C
    D. Class D
    E. Class K

Answer:
E

Knowledge Review

Electrical power lines felled by a tree are lying across a roof, which catches on fire. What classification of fire is this?

    A. Class A
    B. Class B
    C. Class C
    D. Class D
    E. Class K

Answer:
C

Knowledge Review

A candle on a table ignites nearby draperies. What classification of fire is this?

    A. Class A
    B. Class B
    C. Class C
    D. Class D
    E. Class K

Answer:
A

Knowledge Review

Magnesium supplies in a factory ignite when fire spreads from a wastepaper fire. What classification of fire is this?

    A. Class A
    B. Class B
    C. Class C
    D. Class D
    E. Class K

Answer: D

Firefighting Resources

One important reason for identifying the fire classification is to select the most effective means of suppressing the fire.

Four types of firefighting resources are available:

- Portable fire extinguishers
- Interior wet standpipes
- Confinement
- Creative resources

Portable fire extinguishers are widely used on small fires, and we'll cover them in more detail in a moment.

Interior wet standpipes are usually found in commercial and apartment buildings. These devices:

- Usually consist of 100 feet of 1½-inch jacketed hose with a nozzle tip
- Deliver up to 125 gallons of water per minute
- Should be used by three-person teams (one person to handle the hose, one to bleed air from the line, and one to control water pressure)

Visit the Fire Equipment Manufacturers' Association Web site to view animations on how interior wet standpipes work.

The other two firefighting resources focus on actions more than on specific equipment or extinguishing agents.

Confinement as a firefighting resource is based on the fact that confining an interior fire by closing doors to rooms and hallways may help restrict the spread of smoke and heat, and it limits the amount of oxygen available to the fire.

As for creative resources, in terms of firefighting this simply means that in certain circumstances you can make use of the resources at hand to fight fires. Examples:

- Swimming pool or spa water and buckets
- Sand or dirt and shovels
- A garden hose

Portable Fire Extinguishers

For the remainder of this lesson, we'll focus on portable fire extinguishers. As a CERT member, you won't be fighting major fires, but you may put out small ones. And that often means using some type of portable fire extinguisher. The parts of the fire extinguisher are:

- Pin: pulled to activate the extinguisher
- Carrying handle and trigger
- Pressure gauge
- Hose or nozzle
- Cylinder: contains the extinguishing agent

The main types of portable fire extinguishers are:

- Water
- Dry chemical
- Wet chemical
- Carbon dioxide
- Specialized

Each type of portable fire extinguisher is used to extinguish specific classes of fire.

What class of fire do you think a water extinguisher is used on?

Water extinguishers are used on Class A fires.

Standard characteristics include:

- Capacity: 2½ gallons
- Range: 30-40 feet
- Pressure: 110 pounds per square inch (psi)
- Appearance: Usually silver

Dry chemical extinguishers rated for Class B and C fires have a sodium bicarbonate base.

Multipurpose dry chemical extinguishers have a monoammonium phosphate base. They are effective for Class A, B, and C fires. Standard characteristics include:

- Capacity: Approximately 10-20 seconds discharge time
- Range: 8-12 feet
- Pressure: 175-250 psi
- Appearance: Usually red

Wet chemical fire extinguishers are used on Class K fires. These extinguishers are charged with an alkaline mixture that reacts with the burning oils to form a foam-like substance that converts the hot cooking oil or fat into soap.

NOTE: Portable Class K fire extinguishers are intended to supplement the automatic fire extinguishing systems that are installed to cut off the fire's fuel source (natural gas or electricity). They should be used as a follow-up after the automatic fire extinguishing system has deployed.

Carbon dioxide (CO_2) extinguishers, while still in use, are becoming less common. CO_2 extinguishers are used on Class B and C fires. Standard characteristics of a CO_2 extinguisher include:

- Capacity: 8-30 seconds
- Range: 3-8 feet

Specialized extinguishers are also less common. An example is the Class D dry powder extinguisher, which uses special agents to remove oxygen from a Class D fire.

Portable Fire Extinguisher Ratings

Portable fire extinguishers must be rated and approved by the State Fire Marshal and by Underwriters Laboratories.

All portable fire extinguishers have two ratings:

- Fire classification rating – indicates the classes of fire on which the extinguisher is effective
- Capacity rating – indicates the size of fire the extinguisher can handle

Capacity Ratings

On labels for Class A and B extinguishers, the capacity rating is expressed as a number. The larger the number, the larger the fire on which the extinguisher may be used.

The capacity ratings vary among the types of extinguishers, as shown in the chart below.

Extinguisher's Fire Classification Ratings	Capacity Rating
Class A	• Expressed in gallons, from 1 to 40 • 1 = 1 ¼ gallons, 2= 2 ½ gallons, 3= 3 ¾ gallons, etc.
Class B	• Expressed in square feet of coverage, from 1 to 640 • 2 = 2 square feet, etc.
Class C	• No numerical rating • Includes a list of the metals for which the extinguishing agent is effective
Class D	• No numerical rating • Includes a list of the metals for which the extinguishing agent is effective
Class K	• No numerical rating

Choosing the Right Fire Extinguisher

Choosing the right extinguisher for the type of fire you need to put out is critical. Using the wrong type of extinguisher is not only ineffective; it could make a bad situation worse. Check the manufacturer's label to make sure the extinguisher can do the job that you need to get done.

The manufacturer's label displays the extinguisher's ratings and properties, including:

- Type of extinguisher (water, dry chemical, CO_2, or specialized)
- Classification rating (which class of fire the extinguisher is effective on):
    - Class A (ordinary combustibles)
    - Class B (flammable and combustible liquids)
    - Class C (electrical equipment)
    - Class D (combustible metals)

- - Class K (cooking oil or fat)
- Capacity rating (the size of fire the extinguisher can handle)

The chart below summarizes the types of extinguishers that can be used for each class of fire and the methods that each extinguisher uses to put out the fire.

Fire Type	Extinguisher Type	Extinguishing Method
Ordinary Solid Materials (A)	Water	Removes heat
	Foam	Removes air and heat
	Dry chemical	Breaks chain reaction
Flammable Liquids (B)	Foam	Removes air Breaks chain reaction
	CO2	
	Dry chemical	
Electrical Equipment (C)	CO2	Removes air
	Dry chemical	Breaks chain reaction
Combustible Materials (D)	Special agents	Usually remove air
Cooking Oil Fires (K)	Alkaline-mixture (potassium-based liquid)	Removes air

Knowledge Review

A manufacturer's label on a portable fire extinguisher is labeled 3A:40B:C. What is the capacity of this fire extinguisher? Select all that apply.

A. 3 gallons for a Class A fire
B. 3 ¾ gallons for a Class A Fire
C. 4 ¾ gallons for a class B fire
D. 40 square feet for a Class B fire
E. 40 square feet for a Class C fire

Answer:
B and D

Knowledge Review

A portable fire extinguisher with a fire classification rating of ABC can be used to extinguish which of the following fires? Select all that apply.

A. Combustible materials
B. Electrical equipment
C. Flammable liquids
D. Ordinary combustibles

Answer:
B, C, and D

Deciding to Use a Fire Extinguisher

Before attempting to fight any fire with an extinguisher, ask yourself the questions listed on this decision guide.

Can I escape quickly and safely from the area if I attempt to extinguish the fire?
- If the answer is Yes, proceed to the next question.
- If the answer is No, leave immediately!

2. Do I have the right type of extinguisher?
- If the answer is Yes, proceed to the next question.
- If the answer is No, leave immediately!

3. Is the extinguisher large enough for the fire?
- If the answer is Yes, proceed to the next question.
- If the answer is No, leave immediately!

4. Is the area free from other dangers, such as hazardous materials and falling debris?
- If the answer to this question as well as the three preceding ones is Yes, you can attempt to extinguish the fire.
- If the answer is No, leave immediately!

If **ALL** your answers are Yes, you can go ahead and extinguish the fire.

But if **ANY** of your answers are No, do **NOT** try to put out the fire! Instead, leave the building immediately. Shut all doors as you leave to slow the spread of the fire

Decision-Making Scenario

You'll get hands-on practice in using fire suppression techniques when you take the classroom *CERT Basic Training* course.

For now, see if you can apply what you just learned to determine what the classroom CERT members in the following scenario should do.

Ben and Kate are two CERT members assisting in light search and rescue at an office building after a minor earthquake. First, they assess the situation to determine that it's safe to enter the building and to make sure they can quickly and safely exit if necessary. The conditions check out OK, so they enter the building to search for injured survivors.

Inside, in one of the offices, they see a fire in a wastebasket. But before they take any action, they need to consider their own safety.

If they decide to try to put out the fire, are they prepared to escape from the area if anything goes wrong?

   A. Yes
   B. No

Answer:
A

Ben finds a portable fire extinguisher rated for Class A, B, and C fires still securely mounted on the wall near the door of the office. Should he and Kate consider using it to put out the fire?

   A. Yes
   B. No

Answer:
A

Kate checks the label on the extinguisher, which indicates that its capacity is 3-A, 20-B:C. Is the extinguisher large enough for the fire in the wastebasket?

   A. Yes
   B. No

Answer:
A

Ben and Kate quickly scan the area near the wastebasket and see that containers of cleaning products have fallen out of an over-counter cabinet nearby. Several of the containers appear to be damaged, and liquid has spilled out of them onto the floor a few feet from the wastebasket. What should Ben and Kate do next?

   A. Extinguish the fire in the wastebasket, and then clean up the spilled cleaning products
   B. Clean up the spilled cleaning products, and then extinguish the fire in the wastebasket

C. Call their team leader for backup
D. Leave the building immediately

Answer:
D

Lesson Summary

In this lesson, you learned about fire safety fundamentals for CERTs.

Key points covered in this lesson include:

- Fire requires heat, fuel, and oxygen. The combination of these elements can cause a chemical exothermic reaction (fire).
- There are five classes of fire, and they are based on the type of fuel that feeds the fire.
- The type and quantity of fuel dictate the best methods and equipment for extinguishing a fire.
- The decision to extinguish a fire should be based on maintaining your personal safety and having access to the proper resources.

You've completed this lesson. You're now ready to begin Lesson 2-2: Fire Hazards in the Home and Workplace.

Be sure to select Course Menu to exit the lesson and receive credit for the course.

Module 2: Fire Safety
Lesson 2-2: Fire Hazards in the Home and Workplace

Lesson Overview

Welcome to Lesson 2-2: Fire Hazards in the Home and Workplace.

In this lesson, you'll learn about common fire hazards that may exist in your home or workplace and actions you can take to minimize these problems.

After completing this lesson, you should be able to:

- Identify potential fire hazards in your home and workplace
- Identify steps you can take to mitigate fire hazards identified in your home and workplace

It should take you about **30 minutes** to complete this lesson.

Fire Prevention

As in other areas of preparedness and response, CERT fire safety begins at home and at the workplace. Locating potential sources of ignition and taking steps to eliminate or reduce potential fire hazards are simple but highly effective ways to reduce the likelihood of fires.

Many potential fire hazards in the home and at the workplace fall into three categories:

- Electrical hazards
- Natural gas hazards
- Flammable liquids

We'll start with electrical hazards.

Electrical Hazards

Creating electrical hazards in your home is all too easy. You can do it unintentionally as you go about the business of a typically hectic day.

Have you ever been running late, rushed out the front door, and forgotten to turn off an electrical appliance, such as a stove, an oven, or a space heater?

Causes of Electrical Hazards

Forgetting to turn off an electric appliance, such as a stove, oven, or space heater, can create a potential hazard in your home.

In addition, many fire hazards in the home and workplace are caused by electrical overloads and faulty electrical appliances. For example, you can create potential hazards if you:

- Overload electrical outlets
- "Daisy-chain" power strips by plugging one into another
- Use adapters to plug three-prong cords into two-prong outlets
- Use extension cords as permanent wiring
- Place electrical cords under carpets or across high-traffic areas
- Use broken or frayed electrical cords

Knowledge Review

Take a moment now to conduct a mental walk-through of your home, room by room. Make a list of the potential hazards you can think of. Write your answers below and compare to the answers given.

____
____
____
____
____

Answer:
Typical electrical hazards:

- Overloaded electrical outlet
- Power strip without circuit breaker
- "Daisy-chained" power strips
- Heavy appliance (e.g., refrigerator, space heater) plugged into a power strip
- Use of adapter to plug three-prong cord into two-prong outlet
- Grounding prong removed from three-prong extension cord
- Extension cord used as permanent wiring
- Light-duty extension cord used for heavy-duty purpose (e.g., power tool)
- Electrical cord laid under carpet or across high-traffic area
- Broken or frayed electrical cord
- Malfunctioning electrical appliance
- Appliances left on

You should repeat this activity for your workplace. When time permits, conduct actual room-by-room walk-throughs of your home and workplace and add to the lists as necessary.

Knowledge Review

Look at this list of common practices when using electrical devices. Select Safe or Unsafe for each practice to indicate whether it is or isn't safe.

1.   Safe   Unsafe   Placing an electrical cord beneath a rug

2.   Safe   Unsafe   Using a power tool with a heavy-duty extension cord

3.   Safe   Unsafe   Using a three-prong extension cord as permanent wiring for a piece of electrical equipment

4.   Safe   Unsafe   Using a device with a frayed cord

5.   Safe   Unsafe   Plugging a heavy appliance directly into a three-prong wall outlet

6.   Safe   Unsafe   Plugging one power strip into another

Answer:
1. Unsafe
2. Safe
3. Unsafe
4. Unsafe
5. Safe
6. Unsafe

Mitigating Electrical Hazards

Mitigating electrical hazards involves eliminating potentially dangerous situations. Examples:

- Maintain electrical appliances properly: Repair or replace faulty appliances and replace broken or frayed cords.
- Don't run electrical cords under carpets.
- Don't overload outlets.
- Use extension cords only for temporary purposes.

Meeting Your Electrical Needs

I know I'm overloading power strips, but there just aren't enough outlets for all the equipment I need to use! What am I supposed to do?

If you have too few outlets for your electrical needs, you have at least a couple of options.

One: You can simply use the outlets you do have properly, without overloading them. This may mean that you'll need to take a little extra time to get a job done. Leave an appliance unplugged until it is time to use it, then unplug it when you're finished.

Two: If you have other concerns about wiring, you may need to have an electrician do a safety inspection and recommend improvements.

Responding to an Electrical Emergency

Emergencies sometimes occur despite our best efforts. If an electrical emergency occurs, you may have to shut off electricity at the electrical box.

To be prepared to do this:

- Know where the main fuse or circuit breaker is.
- Label power shutoffs for electrical appliances and different parts of your home so that you can turn off specific items or areas if necessary.

Electrical power to a building includes a main switch (for electricity in all the circuits in the building) and individual switches (for electricity in the individual circuits in the building). If you must shut off power to the building, do so in the proper order.

What do you think you should shut off first, the main switch or the individual switches?

The proper order for shutting off power to a building is to shut off all the individual switches BEFORE you shut off the main switch. Proper shutoff procedures differ for circuit breakers and cartridge fuses.

For circuit breakers:
Step 1: Turn off all the individual breakers first.
Step 2: Shut off the main circuit last.

For cartridge fuses:
Step 1: Unscrew all the fuses first.
Step 2: Pull the main fuse out last

When you are certain that it is safe to turn the power back on, reverse the steps (main power first, then individual circuits).

Never enter a flooded basement to shut off the electrical supply. Water conducts electricity!

Knowledge Review

The Greens are remodeling the family basement so they can use it as a hobby and game room. It will be divided into an area where they can use power tools for woodworking projects; an area where they can use amplifiers, an electric guitar, an electric keyboard, and a computer for playing and composing music; and an area where they can use a sewing machine and do crafts projects. What should the Greens do to make sure the remodeled basement will be free of electrical hazards? Select all that apply.

    A. Identify existing electrical hazards in the basement and take appropriate hazard mitigation measures.
    B. Determine the electrical needs for each of the activities that will be performed in the basement.
    C. Install adapters so they can plug three-prong extension cords into two-prong wall outlets in the woodworking and sewing areas
    D. Have an electrician inspect the basement and recommend improvements for safely meeting their electrical needs

Answer:
A, B, and D

Knowledge Review

Look at this list of practices and circle Safe or Unsafe to indicate whether each practice is or is not safe.

1.   Safe Unsafe Plugging a refrigerator into a power strip

2.   Safe Unsafe Plugging a computer and printer into a power strip with a circuit breaker

3.   Safe Unsafe Connecting a bedside lamp to an outlet behind the dresser using an extension cord

4.   Safe Unsafe Turning off electricity by shutting off individual breakers first, and then the main circuit

5.   Safe   Unsafe   Wading through 2 inches of water to the electrical box while wearing rubber boots

Answer:
1. Unsafe
2. Safe
3. Unsafe
4. Safe
5. Unsafe

Natural Gas Hazards

Natural gas is a second category of potential fire hazards.

Natural gas leaking into a home or workplace is hazardous because the gas is:

- An **explosive** substance that can easily be ignited
- An **asphyxiant**, which robs your body of oxygen

What can you do to reduce these hazards?

Mitigating Natural Gas Hazards

You can reduce natural gas hazards if you:

- Install a natural gas detector near your furnace and hot water tank
- Test the detector every month to make sure it works
- Locate and label the gas shutoff valve(s) in your home (There may be multiple gas shutoff valves for appliances inside your house in addition to the main shutoff valve, which is typically located at the gas meter outside the house.)
- Know how to shut off the gas

The procedures for shutting off your home's natural gas are pretty simple …

Gas Shutoff Procedures

You should know where your gas meter is located. You can close most shutoff valves for gas lines to individual appliances by simply turning the valve lever clockwise (to the right) by hand.

To close the main shutoff valve, you usually need to use a non-sparking shutoff wrench.

- Keep the wrench in a specific place near the main shutoff valve, so you can quickly get to the wrench when you need it.
- Use the wrench to turn the shutoff valve clockwise one-quarter turn.
- When the valve is closed, its lever will be positioned perpendicular to the gas line.

Once you have turned off the gas supply, **leave it off**. Only a trained technician can restore gas service.

Responding to a Natural Gas Emergency

In a disaster, check for signs of a natural gas problem, which may exist if:

- You smell gas
- A natural gas detector indicates the presence of gas
- The indicator on the gas meter shows that gas is still flowing when all gas appliances and heat are turned off

In these situations:

- Do NOT use the phone, light switch, or anything that could ignite the gas.
- Turn off the gas supply at the meter **outside the building**.
- Never enter the basement of a burning structure to turn off any utility.

Knowledge Review

Joe's wife says she smells gas on the deck at the back of the house. Joe joins her on the deck and agrees that he smells gas, too. He then checks the gas meter outside the house. The odor of gas at the meter is stronger than it was on the deck, and the meter shows that gas is flowing. What should Joe do?

A. Close the main shutoff valve at the gas meter outside of the house
B. Go inside the house immediately and phone the gas company to report a leak
C. Spray water on the gas supply piping coming out of the ground below the gas meter
D. Have his wife close the shutoff valves on the gas appliances inside the house while he closes the main shutoff valve outside the house

Answer:
A

Flammable Liquid Hazards

The third category of potential fire hazards you need to be aware of is flammable liquids. Many common household and office products are flammable or combustible. For simplicity, we'll refer to both flammable and combustible liquids simply as flammable liquids.

Flammable liquids can ignite with explosive force. The vapors — not the liquid itself — can be ignited by any open flame (a match, cigarette, or pilot light), spark, or even static electricity.

flammable: *flammable liquids have a flash point below 100ºF. They are capable of being easily ignited and of burning quickly*

combustible: *combustible liquids have a flashpoint at or above 100º F. They are less hazardous than flammable liquids but still pose a risk*

Common Flammable Liquid Products

Examples of flammable liquids commonly found in the home and workplace include:

- Gasoline
- Kerosene
- Oil
- Charcoal lighter fluid
- Paint thinners and removers
- Acetone
- Spot removers and cleaning fluids
- Solvents
- Cleaning products

Products packaged as aerosols (e.g., deodorants, hair sprays, insecticides, spray paint) can also pose a hazard if they become heated, because they contain flammable propellants.

Mitigating Flammable Liquid Hazards

To minimize hazards associated with flammable liquid products:

- Read labels to identify flammable products.
- Store flammable products properly in approved safety containers, away from living areas.
- Use flammable liquids in a well-ventilated area.
- In case of fire, use a portable fire extinguisher rated for Class B fires.

Storing Flammable Liquids

Because of their volatility, flammable liquid products require special storage and handling. To ensure safe storage of these products, remember the acronym LIES.

- *L*imit: Limit the amount of flammable liquids in storage.
- *I*solate: Isolate products in approved containers stored in enclosed cabinets. Protect them from ignition sources. Don't store flammable liquids in a mechanical room. Never bring gasoline indoors.
- *E*liminate: Eliminate products that are no longer necessary by disposing of them properly. Reduce fumes by practicing good housekeeping — wipe up spills immediately.
- *S*eparate: Separate incompatible materials (e.g., don't store flammables near corrosives).

Knowledge Review

Which of these people are following safe practices for storing and handling flammable liquids? Select all that apply.

A. Jake keeps only enough paint thinner on hand for the project he's currently working on.
B. Bonnie keeps combustible cleaning fluid in a closed cupboard.
C. Janet stores flammable products in a cabinet that is separate from the one in which she stores corrosives.
D. Carl stores gasoline in a metal container in the basement of his house.

Answer:
A, B, and C

General Fire Prevention Strategies

Eliminating fire hazards associated with electricity, natural gas, and flammable liquids will go a long way toward reducing fire risks. There are many other ways you can improve fire safety in your home and workplace. Write your answers below and compare to the answers given.

____
____
____
____
____

Answer:

- Install smoke alarms.
- Conduct a home (and workplace) hazard hunt.
- Inspect wood stoves and chimneys annually.
- Purchase only space heaters that have been laboratory tested and approved, and follow the manufacturer's directions when using them.
- Keep combustible materials at least 3 feet away from heat sources.
- Keep matches and lighters away from children.
- Never leave fire unattended.

Consult the general fire prevention strategies list for additional detail about each of the strategies.

General Fire Prevention Strategies

Install smoke alarms on every level of your home and near all sleeping areas.
Conduct a home (and workplace) hazard hunt. Many items and conditions around the home and workplace can pose fire hazards. Taking time to look for and eliminate hazards will reduce the risk.
Inspect wood stoves and chimneys annually. Burning wood leaves flammable creosote deposits in the firebox, flue, and chimney. These buildups must be removed professionally to minimize the risk of fire.
Purchase only space heaters that have been laboratory tested and approved. Follow the manufacturer's directions for use. Plug heaters directly into a wall socket, and unplug them when they are not in use.
Keep combustible materials away from heat sources, including stoves, heaters, candles, and fireplaces. Materials such as curtains, bedding, furniture, towels, clothing, bags, and boxes can catch fire quickly. Keep them at least 3 feet away from heat sources.
Keep matches and lighters away from children. Children are fascinated by fire and will play with matches and lighters if they are available.
Never leave fire unattended. A controlled fire can quickly become uncontrolled.

Never leave a candle, fireplace, or space heater unattended.

You should also use this fire hazard mitigation checklist for your home. Then, fill it out, indicating whether you have completed each mitigation step. Bring your completed checklist with you for discussion when you attend the CERT classroom training.

Fire Hazard Mitigation Checklist

Electrical Hazard Mitigation	YES	NO
Eliminate electrical outlet overloads.		
Ensure that all power strips have circuit breakers.		
Avoid using power strips or extension cords in series.		
Plug heavy appliances directly into wall outlets (not power strips)		
Eliminate three-prong/two-prong adapters.		
Replace long-term use of extension cords with permanent wiring.		
Have a heavy-duty extension cord available for power tools.		
Avoid electrical cords under carpets or across high-traffic areas.		
Replace broken or frayed electrical cords.		
Repair or replace faulty electrical appliances.		
Know how and where to shut off electrical power.		
Contact an electrician for electrical improvements (if needed).		
Have a Class C or ABC fire extinguisher available.		
Natural Gas Hazard Mitigation	**YES**	**NO**
Install a natural gas monitor.		
Test monitor monthly.		
Know how and where to shut off gas.		
Label gas meter shutoff valves.		
Store shutoff wrench near gas meter.		
Install a natural gas monitor.		
Flammable Liquids Hazard Mitigation	**YES**	**NO**
Identify flammable products (read labels).		
Keep flammables in approved safety containers.		
Use flammable liquids only in well-ventilated areas.		
Store flammable liquids in a fireproof cabinet away from living areas.		
Eliminate sources of ignition near flammables.		
Wipe up spills immediately to reduce fumes.		
Separate incompatible materials (flammables and corrosives).		
Have a Class B or ABC fire extinguisher available.		

When you are done with home mitigation, make a list of mitigation tasks that need to be completed at your workplace.

Lesson Summary

In this lesson, you learned about actions that you can take to minimize fire hazards in your home and workplace.

Key points covered in this lesson include:

- A CERT member's fire safety role begins at home and at the workplace.
- Electricity, natural gas, and flammable liquids can create fire hazards.
- Taking the time to look for and eliminate fire hazards reduces the risk of fire in the home or workplace.

You've completed this lesson. You're now ready to begin Lesson 2-3: Safe Fire Suppression.

Module 2: Fire Safety
Lesson 2-3: Safe Fire Suppression

Lesson Overview

Welcome to Lesson 2-3: Safe Fire Suppression.

In this lesson, you'll learn about steps and procedures for safely suppressing fires. Later, when you take the classroom-based *CERT Basic Training* course, you will be trained in how to <u>perform </u>these procedures.

After completing this lesson, you should be able to:

- Identify safe practices for fire suppression
- State the steps of the PASS procedure for fire extinguisher operation

It should take about **25 minutes** to complete this lesson.

Fire Safety Rules

As discussed in the previous lesson, there may be circumstances in which, once you have completed the classroom-based CERT training, you would be able to suppress small fires. However, when carrying out this role, you need to follow some basic guidelines to protect your own safety.

Specifically, there are eight basic rules for safe fire suppression. Let's look at them one by one.

Rule 1: Use personal safety equipment (sometimes called PPE, for "personal protective equipment") to protect yourself.

The basic personal safety equipment that CERT members wear in a disaster includes:

- Gloves
- Goggles
- Dust mask
- Helmet
- Sturdy shoes or boots

Rule 2: Don't try to fight a fire alone.

In a disaster, there is safety in numbers, so be sure that you have help.

- Work with a buddy. Your buddy covers your back, looks around for danger, and protects your safety.
- Have a backup team whenever possible. Having a backup team covering you and your buddy just makes good sense. The backup team can support your fire suppression efforts and can provide help if you need it.

Always keep in mind that your first priority is your personal safety. Don't put yourself at risk!

Rule 3: Check before entering.

This involves doing a sizeup of the situation. Sizeup is a nine-step process of gathering facts and analyzing the situation to determine if it's safe for you to help, and, if so, how you can best be of assistance.

The nine steps in sizeup are:

1. Gather the facts.
2. Assess and communicate the damage.
3. Consider probabilities.
4. Assess your own situation.
5. Establish priorities.
6. Make decisions.
7. Develop plans of action.
8. Take action.
9. Evaluate progress.

The sizeup process applies to many types of CERT operations. You can learn more about it in the classroom-based CERT training.

Sizeup for fire suppression specifically includes the following precautions before you enter an area where there might be a fire:

- Feel closed doors with the back of your hand, working from the bottom of the door up. Do NOT touch the door handle before feeling the door.
- If the door is hot, there is a fire behind it. **Do not enter!** Opening the door will feed additional oxygen to the fire. Trapped fuel vapors can ignite violently.
- Do not enter smoke-filled areas. Fire suppression in smoke-filled areas requires breathing and protective equipment that CERTs don't have.

Rule 4: Plan your exit.

- Always have two ways to exit the fire area. A backup escape plan is necessary in case your main escape route becomes blocked.
- Whenever possible, as you leave the area, shut doors behind you to confine the fire.

Flames spread much faster than you might think. To see how quickly a fire can progress, select the Play button to the right.

Knowledge Review

When checking for survivors in a storm-damaged building, CERT member buddies Greg and Sean encounter a room that has its door slightly ajar and smoke coming out into the hallway. What should they do?

- A. Check the door temperature before entering the room
- B. Enter the room and stay low
- C. Not enter the room and shut the door, if possible, then leave the building
- D. Put on supplied-air respirators before entering the room

Answer: C

Fire Safety Rules

Rule 5: Maintain a safe distance and position in relation to the fire.

- Don't get too close. If you try to put out a small fire, know the effective range of your fire extinguisher. Stay near the outer boundary of that range.
- If you feel the heat before discharging the extinguisher, you're too close. Move up on the fire as it gets smaller to the point of extinguishment.
- Stay low to the ground. Smoke will naturally rise. Keeping low to the ground will provide you with fresher air to breathe.
- Remember: If smoke is filling up a room, confine the fire, if possible, and leave the building.

Knowledge Review

A box of rags has caught on fire in Dan's garage. Fortunately, he has a portable fire extinguisher on hand that is effective on this class of fire. How should he position himself to safely fight the fire? Select all that apply.

A. He should stand upright and avoid getting low to the ground.
B. He should position himself near the limit of his extinguisher's effective range.
C. He should move in just close enough to the fire to feel its heat.
D. He should move up on the fire as it grows smaller to the point of being extinguished

Answer:
B and D

Fire Safety Rules

Rule 6: Suppress only small fires.
A small fire is about the size of a wastepaper can, and it can be extinguished with one fire extinguisher.

Learn the capability of your equipment (capacity rating of your fire extinguisher). Do not try to suppress a fire that is too large for your equipment.

Rule 7: Use the correct equipment in the correct manner.

First, select the right equipment.

Select a fire extinguisher that:

- Is rated for the class of fire to be extinguished
- Has the capacity for the size of fire to be extinguished
- Is of a size and weight that you can effectively hold and operate

Remember: Types of portable fire extinguishers and their fire classification and capacity ratings are covered in lesson 2-1: Introduction to Fire Safety.

Second, know the proper procedure for operating a portable fire extinguisher.

An easy way to remember the steps of the procedure is to use the acronym PASS, which stands for...

The PASS Procedure

Simply put, the PASS procedure stands for:

- **P**ull
- **A**im
- **S**queeze
- **S**weep

Step	Action
Pull	First, pull the safety pin in the handle (twist to break the seal).
Aim	Next, test the fire extinguisher to be sure it works and then aim the hose or nozzle at the base of the fire.
Squeeze	Third, squeeze the trigger.
Sweep	Finally, sweep the base of the fire from side to side. Be sure to hold the extinguisher in an upright position as you sweep. Tip: When using a water extinguisher, be careful to avoid scattering lightweight material with the pressurized water, which could spread the fire.

Knowledge Review

CERT members Lauren and Louise have encountered a small combustible metals fire in an industrial process plant that has been damaged by an electrical storm. They are wearing personal safety gear – including helmets, goggles, gloves, and sturdy shoes or boots – and they have a Class ABC portable fire extinguisher at hand. What should they do?

   A. Use the fire extinguisher that they have, but allow extra distance from the fire for increased safety
   B. Split up and have one person stay with the fire while the other leaves to get the right equipment to safety suppress it
   C. Make sure the y have two escape routes, and then try to put out the fire with the extinguisher that they have
   D. Leave the area

Answer:
D

Fire Safety Rules

Rule 8: Overhaul the fire.

Overhauling is the process of locating any potential sources of re-ignition, such as hidden burning material, and extinguishing them. Always overhaul fires to make sure that they're really and truly out before you move on!

CAUTION: Safe fire suppression requires training and practice! You can get hands-on instruction in the how-to's for operating a fire extinguisher properly and putting out small fires safely in the CERT classroom-based training.

There are some special concerns you should be aware of when it comes to suppressing and overhauling Class K fires (cooking oils and fat in commercial kitchens).

Class K fires are particularly difficult to extinguish because they tend to re-ignite. For this reason, only an extinguisher with a Class K rating is recommended for use on this type of fire.

Also, you should first activate the cooking appliance fire suppression system (installed in commercial kitchens) BEFORE using a Class K portable fire extinguisher. Activating the fire suppression system cuts off the fuel source (natural gas or electricity) for the fire and then blankets the hot cooking oil with thick foam produced by the agent contained in the extinguishing system. You should then use the portable extinguisher for follow-up, if needed.

Knowledge Review

Place the following steps for operating a portable fire extinguisher in the correct order, from first to last.

____ Test the extinguisher and aim the hose or nozzle at the base of the fire.
____ Squeeze the trigger.
____ Pull the safety pin.
____ Sweep the base of the fire from side to side.

Answer:
2, 3, 1, 4

Knowledge Review

CERT members Marty and Lee encountered a small fire in a home that had been damaged during a storm. They made sure that they had the right equipment for the job and that it was safe for them to extinguish the fire. Then, using a portable fire extinguisher, they soon extinguished the fire. What should they do next?

    A. Open all doors to let in fresh air
    B. Exit as quickly as possible
    C. Overhaul the fire
    D. Empty the extinguisher's canister

Answer:
C

Lesson Summary

In this lesson, you learned about actions that CERTs can take to suppress fires safely.

Key points covered in this lesson focused on how to protect your safety when suppressing fires.

- Wear protective equipment.
- Work with a buddy and as a team.
- Plan for safe entry and exit.
- Maintain a safe distance and position in relation to the fire.
- Suppress only small fires using the proper equipment.
- Use the PASS procedure to operate fire extinguishers.
- Overhaul the fire to prevent re-ignition.

You've completed this lesson.

CAUTION!!

Although you have completed this lesson on fire suppression, remember that you have not been trained to perform CERT functions. Proper training requires classroom-based instruction and supervised practice.

Do **NOT** try to use the procedures introduced in this lesson until you have completed the *CERT Basic Training* course or other supervised training on the use of fire extinguishers.

For now, let's review what you learned in this module and then see what you can expect to learn in the next module.

Module Summary

In Module 2: Fire Safety, you learned about the fire safety practices that CERTs must follow.

Key points included:

- Fire requires heat, fuel, and oxygen. The combination of these elements can cause a chemical exothermic reaction (fire).
- There are five classes of fire, and they are based on the type of fuel that feeds the fire.
- The type and quantity of fuel dictate the best methods and equipment for extinguishing a fire.
- The decision to extinguish a fire should be based on maintaining your personal safety and having access to the proper resources.
- A CERT member's fire safety role begins at home and at the workplace.
- Electricity, natural gas, and flammable liquids can create fire hazards.
- Taking the time to look for and eliminate fire hazards reduces the risk of having a fire in the home or workplace.
- Wear protective equipment.
- Work with a buddy and as a team.
- Plan for safe entry and exit.
- Maintain a safe distance and position in relation to the fire.
- Suppress only small fires using the proper equipment.
- Use the PASS procedure to operate a fire extinguisher.
- Overhaul the fire to prevent re-ignition.

What's Next?

Now that you've completed this module, you're ready to move on to Module 3: Hazardous Materials and Terrorist Incidents. In that module, you'll learn about practices that CERTs must follow in situations that involve hazardous materials or terrorism. You'll find out how to determine if hazardous materials are present and actions you can take to deal with hazardous materials safely. You'll also learn about what you can do to prepare for and respond to a possible terrorist attack.

Module 3: Hazardous Materials and Terrorist Incidents
Lesson 3-1: Introduction to Special Situations

Module Overview

Welcome to Module 3: Hazardous Materials and Terrorist Incidents.

Hazardous materials and terrorist incidents are two special situations that you may encounter as a CERT member. Both scenarios have unique dangers associated with them; to best protect yourself and others, you need to be aware of these perils.

In this module, you'll learn about the special dangers associated with hazardous materials and terrorist incidents, and you'll learn about the CERT protocol that you must follow to help keep everyone safe.

You'll also see how hazardous materials and terrorist incidents often come hand in hand.

It should take you about **1 hour 5 minutes** to complete the three lessons in this module:

- Lesson 3-1: Introduction to Special Situations — **15 minutes**
- Lesson 3-2: Hazardous Materials Safety — **20 minutes**
- Lesson 3-3: Terrorism and CERT — **30 minutes**

After completing this module, you should be able to:

- Identify practices that CERTs must follow in situations that involve hazardous materials or terrorism

Lesson Overview

Welcome to Lesson 3-1: Introduction to Special Situations.

In this lesson, you'll learn about the types of situations that may involve hazardous materials or terrorism and the procedures that CERTs follow in such situations.

After completing this lesson, you should be able to:

- Identify special situations as incidents involving hazardous materials and/or terrorism

- Identify practices that CERTs must follow for hazardous materials and terrorist incidents

It should take you about **15 minutes** to complete this lesson.

Hazardous Materials Defined

First of all, it's important to know what hazardous materials are. They're part of our daily lives and can often be found in the home, in the workplace, in other commercial locations, and on the highway.

It can be difficult to remember how risky some of these materials are, because we're in daily contact with them. But when they're mishandled, these materials can be very dangerous to us, our property, and our environment.

Hazardous materials are materials that:

- Corrode other materials
- Explode or are easily ignited
- React strongly with water
- Are unstable when exposed to heat or shock
- Are toxic to humans, animals, or the environment

How Are Terrorism and Hazardous Materials Related?

Simply put, terrorism and hazardous materials are related because most terrorist acts involve some kind of hazardous material.

All weapons of mass destruction (WMD) are hazardous materials. They might include:

- Chemical agents
- Biological agents
- Radiological and nuclear materials
- Explosives

We'll return to terrorist incidents later in the module.

CERT Special Situation Response

Despite what you'll learn in the classroom *for CERT Basic Training*, you won't have enough training to respond to situations that involve hazardous materials.

In fact, CERT members are never asked to respond to any incidents involving hazardous materials. Safety is always the first priority in these situations, and it requires extensive training and special equipment to contain, clean up, and dispose of hazardous materials.

Knowledge Review

What are some characteristics of hazardous materials? Select all that apply.

> A. They can be safely disposed of in rivers and streams
> B. If spilled, they can be cleaned up by trained CERT members.
> C. They corrode other materials.
> D. They may explode or combust easily.
> E. They are toxic to humans and animals.

Answer:
C, D, E

Reacting to Special Situations

How should you deal with situations that involve hazardous materials?

You should treat all known and suspected hazardous materials as STOP signs — in other words, do not attempt to respond under any circumstances.

Instead, complete your evaluation of the situation from a safe distance:

- Don't touch anything
- Position yourself uphill and upwind from the incident
- Warn others to stay away from the area

After evaluating the situation, what should you do next?

Informing Emergency Responders

Once you are safe, you should call 911!

Knowledge Review

When calling 911, what sort of information do you think you should provide to the operator? Write your answers below and compare to the answers given.

____
____
____
____
____

Answer:
Provide as much information as you can about:

- What appears to have happened
- Where it happened
- What is happening now
- The number and types of known injuries
- Who you are
- Where you are
- How you can be reached

Knowledge Review

A tanker truck has crashed and spilled an unknown hazardous material across the highway. Where should you go to safely call 911?

A. Inside your car, with the doors shut and the windows rolled up.
B. The nearest highway exit
C. Uphill and upwind from the spill
D. The cabin of the overturned truck, after checking the driver for injuries

Answer:
C

Knowledge Review

Chemical or radiological materials are especially hazardous to people in the immediate vicinity, because these materials easily contaminate clothes and skin and can cause permanent damage.

If you find that you have been exposed to these materials, what should you do?

A. Douse yourself with the nearest source of water, and then blot dry.
B. Call 911 immediately to inform emergency responders of the location and nature of the disaster.
C. Leave the contaminated area immediately, get upwind and uphill from the hazard, and wait for professional responders.
D. Run uphill and upwind, and tell everyone else in the area to do the same.

Answer:

C

Contamination

While you wait for professional responders, you can use some basic decontamination procedures:

- Remove everything, including jewelry.
- Cut off any clothing that is usually removed over the head.
- Wash your hands, using any source of available cool water and soap.
- Flush your entire body with cool water.
- Blot yourself dry; do not rub.
- Put on clean clothes if available.
- Wait in safe area for professional responders to arrive.

Now that you have reduced your own risk of injury, how can you help the rest of the people affected by the disaster?

Helping Others

Never attempt to treat survivors inside the contamination zone. The best thing you can do for other people is to tell them to **leave the area**.

Once the area has been evacuated, explain the basic decontamination process and caution survivors to wait for responders who will perform a thorough decontamination.

Remember that your personal safety is **always** the first priority during a hazardous materials or terrorist incident. Without the special training and equipment required to respond to these situations, the most helpful thing you can do is avoid becoming injured yourself.

You'll learn more about procedures following a chemical release in Lesson 3 of this module.

Knowledge Review

Now that you've gone through this introduction to special situations, let's see what you remember!

Use your knowledge of hazardous materials and terrorist incidents to pick out which of the following statements are true and which are false.

1.   T   F   CERT members are qualified to respond to terrorist incidents after completing this training and the classroom training.

2.   T   F   During situations that involve hazardous materials, your own safety is your first priority.

3.   T   F   Weapons of mass destruction (WMD) are all hazardous materials.

4.   T   F   Immediately treat anyone exposed to a chemical or biological threat and stay close to others in the impacted area.

Answer:
1. F
2. T
3. T
4. F

Lesson Summary

In this lesson, you learned the basics about special situations.

Key points covered in this lesson include:

- Treat hazardous materials as STOP signs: Only professional responders with special equipment are trained to deal with these situations.
- If you become contaminated, use standard decontamination procedures and then wait for responders to perform complete decontamination.

You've completed this lesson. You're now ready to begin Lesson 3-2: Hazardous Materials Safety.

Module 3: Hazardous Materials and Terrorist Incidents
Lesson 3-2: Hazardous Materials Safety

Lesson Overview

Welcome to Lesson 3-2: Hazardous Materials Safety.

In this lesson, you'll learn about common hazardous materials, their properties, and their potential dangers. You'll also learn how to safely use and store these materials in your home.

After completing this lesson, you should be able to:

- Identify means you can use to determine if hazardous materials are present
- Identify what CERT members should do in situations involving hazardous materials

It should take about **20 minutes** to complete this lesson.

Knowledge Review

Chemicals are part of our daily lives. We use them to clean our homes and to fix machinery, and we store them in our homes. Chemicals are used and/or stored in many locations in every community.

In fact, we're so used to having chemicals around that we sometimes forget how dangerous they can be. Chemicals pose a health and environmental threat when mixed, spilled, or used improperly. It's important to handle, store, and dispose of them safely. Can you think of any potentially hazardous chemicals you have in your home? Write your answers below and compare to the answers given.

____
____
____
____
____

Answer:
Common household chemicals may include:
- Bleach
- Ammonia
- Acid (drain cleaner, batteries)

- Antifreeze
- Chlorine
- Disinfectants
- Detergents
- Alkaline products (oven cleaner, batteries)

Preventing Disaster

Products containing hazardous materials can be found in nearly every home (such as the hairspray bottle in the image at right). These products can be dangerous. But most chemical accidents are preventable if you simply take the time to read product labels and learn how to use the products correctly.

However, if an accident does happen, you need to know what to do. By immediately taking the appropriate action during a hazardous materials emergency, you can reduce the risk of injury.

Responding to Disaster

When CERT members respond to a disaster, their assessment must determine whether hazardous materials are present and what type of danger the materials pose. But everyone should know the basic steps to take if there's a hazardous materials emergency at home or work.

As we discussed in the previous lesson, materials are considered hazardous if they:

- Corrode other materials
- Explode or are easily ignited
- React strongly with water
- Are unstable when exposed to heat or shock
- Are toxic to humans, animals, or the environment

What should you do if you suspect or discover that someone has been exposed to hazardous materials?

You should gauge your reaction based on the type of exposure and the type of chemicals involved. Some household hazardous materials are dangerous when they're ingested or absorbed through the skin. Others are harmful only when they're inhaled. This is another good reason to read product labels: Besides explaining how to use a chemical, they describe its possible dangers.

To determine if someone has been exposed, watch his or her symptoms carefully. A person exposed to hazardous materials may have one or several of the following symptoms:

- Difficulty breathing
- Changes in skin color
- Headaches, blurred vision, dizziness
- Cramps or diarrhea
- Clumsiness or lack of coordination
- Irritation of the eyes, skin, throat, or respiratory tract

Knowledge Review

Let's see what you already know. Review the following actions involving hazardous materials. Which do you think would be considered safe practices? Which would be considered unsafe?

1. Safe Unsafe You notice the smell of gas coming from the kitchen. You leave the house and move your family to a neighbor's house, where you can call for help.

2. Safe Unsafe To do your part for the environment, you always save old containers. You use them to store household cleaning solutions.

3. Safe Unsafe The carbon monoxide detector in your home goes off. You leave the house and move your family to the nearest upwind, uphill location.

4. Safe Unsafe You keep a candle lit as you clean the kitchen because the smell of the chemicals is too strong.

Answer:
   1. Safe
   2. Unsafe
   3. Safe
   4. Unsafe

If an Emergency Occurs

If you determine that someone has been exposed to a chemical, there are three possible courses of action you can take. Each depends on the type of exposure and the type of chemical involved.

If a poison is ingested find the original container and call the poison control center (800-222-1222) immediately. Follow the directions you are given.

If a chemical gets into the eyes flush with water for at least 15 minutes. If possible, have someone else call 911.

If there is danger of fire or explosion get out of the building immediately. When you are safely outside and away from danger, call the fire department. Remain uphill and upwind from the building.

Protect Yourself!

There are also many steps you can take to **prevent** hazardous materials accidents before they happen. Recall from Module 2: Fire Safety that you can use a simple acronym to protect yourself in your home: LIES

The LIES practices will help keep you and your family safe:

- **L**imit the amount of hazardous materials that you have stored.
- **I**solate products in approved containers, and protect them from sources of ignition.
- **E**liminate products that are no longer necessary by disposing of them properly.
- **S**eparate incompatible materials.

What other ways can you think of to avoid hazardous material emergencies?

Knowledge Review

The following statements concern appropriate actions related to hazardous material situations. Based on the safety measures we've covered so far, decide which statements are true and which are false.

1.   T   F   If there is danger that a household chemical may catch fire or explode, you should clean it up quickly.

2.   T   F   If you suspect that a child has ingested a chemical, you should administer milk of magnesia to help him or her expel it.

3.   T   F   If a chemical enters your eyes, you should immediately flush them with water.

4.   T   F   Chemicals must be kept away from any heat source or open flame.

Answer:
1. F
2. F
3. T
4. T

Natural Gas and Carbon Monoxide Hazards

If you use natural gas in your home for cooking and heating, you should be aware of its hazards and be aware of potential leaks.

Gas companies often add an odor to gas to alert you when there is a leak. It usually smells like rotten eggs. Other signs to alert you to a leak are blowing dirt or dust, bubbles forming in a glass of water, and a hissing or whistling noise.

There is no device that will detect a natural gas leak. However, there are devices that will alert you to another potential risk: carbon monoxide (CO) poisoning. CO is produced by the incomplete burning of solid, liquid, and gaseous fuels. CO is colorless, tasteless, and odorless. You can install a carbon monoxide detector that will let you know if you are at risk of CO poisoning.

Identifying Hazardous Materials in Storage

Hazardous materials are stored in many places throughout your community. You may find them in production facilities, storage tanks, warehouses, schools, office buildings, places of worship, and many retailers such as supermarkets and hardware stores.

To identify locations where significant quantities of hazardous materials are used or stored and inform people about the materials they contain, the National Fire Protection Association (NFPA) developed the NFPA 704 Diamond.

The NFPA 704 Diamond

The NFPA 704 Diamond is divided into four colored quadrants that provide information about the material stored inside the given facility. These quadrants create a standard system for identifying hazards.

Each color in the diamond represents a specific type of hazard:

- Blue represents a health hazard.
- Red represents flammability.

- Yellow represents reactivity.
- White provides information about special precautions.

There's a number in each of the colored quadrants of the NFPA 704 Diamond. These numbers always range from 1 to 4 and represent the degree of danger that is associated with the stored material.

The higher the number, the higher the risk!

But what about the white quadrant?

The White Quadrant

The white quadrant of the diamond uses a symbol instead of a number to convey information.

These different symbols represent different types of hazards:

- W indicates a material that shows unusual reactivity with water
- OX indicates a material that reacts violently with oxygen

Magnesium is one example of a material that would be indicated by a white quadrant W. Ammonium nitrate is an example of a substance that would be indicated by an OX.

Next, we'll talk about what you should do when you see an NFPA 704 Diamond.

Encountering a Diamond

The NFPA 704 Diamond is placed on placards to indicate hazardous materials inside a location, something that can be pretty scary after a disaster. Chemicals may have spilled or leaked, presenting a danger to people in the vicinity.

So what do CERT members do when they encounter one of these placards and they see or smell signs that the hazardous materials may no longer be properly contained?

CERT members should consider the NFPA 704 Diamond placard a **stop sign.**

In fact, in the immediate aftermath of a disaster, the **only** action CERT members should take when a facility is labeled with an NFPA Diamond and there are signs that hazardous materials are leaking is to warn people of the danger and evacuate them to an upwind and uphill location.

You'll learn more about how to recognize the signs of large-scale hazardous material emergencies in the classroom-based *CERT Basic Training* course.

Knowledge Review

1.   T   F   The blue quadrant represents special precautions.

2.   T   F   The red quadrant represents reactivity.

3.   T   F   The yellow quadrant represents reactivity.

4.   T   F   The blue quadrant represents health hazards.

Answer:
   1. F
   2. F
   3. T
   4. T

Identifying Hazardous Materials in Transit

The NFPA placard identifies hazardous materials in fixed locations. The U.S. Department of Transportation (DOT) has developed a placard system of its own to identify hazardous materials in transit.

DOT placards:
- Use a combination of colors, symbols, and numbers
- Indicate hazardous materials being carried in the placarded vehicle or railcar

The DOT placard system:

Name	Color
1.1 Explosives	Orange
2 Flammable Gas	Red
2 Inhalation Hazard	White
3 Flammable	Red
4 Flammable Solid	Red and White
4 Spontaneously Combustible	Red and White
4 Dangerous When Wet	Blue

5.1 Oxidizer	Yellow
6 Poison	White
7 Radioactive	Yellow and White
8 Corrosive	Black and White

This system is just one of three placard systems that you may encounter.

Placard Systems

The DOT placard system is the most commonly used in the United States, but there are two other placard systems that you might see occasionally:

- The United Nations (UN) system, which is used internationally as well as in the United States
- The North American (NA) system, which is currently being phased out but is still sometimes used on shipments from Canada

Protect Yourself

Use extreme caution when you are near any vehicle accident, because DOT placards are not foolproof.

- They are required only for more than 1,001 pounds of hazardous materials — meaning that, even if the vehicle does not have a placard, it may still be extremely dangerous!
- Sometimes drivers forget to change the placard when they change their cargo, resulting in falsely marked or absent placards.

Knowledge Review

Name three placarding systems that you may encounter in the United States.

____
____
____
____
____

Answer:
Common placarding systems in the US include:

- NFPA 704 diamond
- Department of Transportation (DOT) Placard System
- United Nations (UN) System
- North American (NA) System

Explaining the DOT Placard

The top, middle, and bottom sections of a DOT placard each contain important information.

- The **top portion** of the placard contains a symbol representing the hazard that is associated with the material. In this case, the symbol indicates that fire is a hazard.
- The **middle portion** of the placard often contains text that provides a hazard description for the material. In this case, it indicates that the material is an oxidizer (a chemical that supplies its own oxygen and helps other combustible material burn more readily).
- In many cases, the **bottom portion** of the placard contains a number that identifies the DOT hazard class that applies to the material.

Hazardous Materials Scenario

The Harper family – Paul, Elisabeth, Claire, and Allie – spent the afternoon playing Frisbee in their yard and are now heading back inside to do some chores around the house. As they do simple tasks such as cooking, paying bills, and cleaning, they may come in contact with hazardous materials. You can help them make smart decisions by answering some questions about their activities and actions.

Scenario Question 1

Paul is in the kitchen cooking while Allie plays on the floor nearby. There are several potential hazards in the room. Which of the following are potential chemical hazards Paul should be aware of?

A. Open cabinet under sink containing cleaning supplies
B. Cleaning supplies on counter beside stove
C. Cleaning product containers in trash can
D. Spilled cleaning product on counter

Answer:
A, B, C, D

Scenario Question 2

As Allie plays on the floor, a cabinet full of cleaning supplies is close by. Looking more closely at the chemicals in the cabinet, you can see that Allie could easily get into them. What is the proper way to store these chemicals?

    A. All together in a locked cabinet
    B. Outside of the home, in a shed or garage
    C. According to individual labels

Answer:
C

Scenario Question 3

Paul has set this cleaner by the stove. Is this a hazard?

    A. Yes
    B. No

Answer:
A

Scenario Question 4

Paul has thrown this container in the trash can. Do you think this is disposed of properly?

    A. Yes, if they are safe enough to keep in the house, you can throw them out with everything else.
    B. No, you should never throw containers away in regular garbage.
    C. I'm not sure, I would need more information to make a decision.

Answer:
C

Scenario Question 5

Paul has accidentally spilled a chemical on the counter. Without knowing what this chemical is, what should you do with the spill?

    A. Leave it, the damage has been done.
    B. Clean it with the rag immediately.
    C. Leave the building.

Answer:
B

Scenario Question 6

While Paul and Allie are in the kitchen, Elisabeth is in the basement paying bills. As she works, she thinks she smells gas. An odor is often the first thing people notice in a gas leak. In addition to an odor, what are other signs of a gas leak?

    A. Visible white cloud
    B. Cold furnace
    C. Blowing dirt or dust
    D. Hissing or whistling noise
    E. Sparks coming from radiator
    F. Bubbles forming in a glass of water

Answer:
C, D, and F

Scenario Question 7

If the gas odor is strong, like rotten eggs, it may be a serious leak. If it's a serious leak, what should Elisabeth do first?

    A. Open the windows.
    B. Turn off the gas.
    C. Gather her family and leave.
    D. Call for help.

Answer:
C

Scenario Question 8

Because of the strong odor, Elisabeth and her family are leaving the house. As they are leaving, Elisabeth realizes that several appliances are on, as well as the overhead lights. What should she do?

    A. Turn off everything.
    B. Leave them on.
    C. Turn off the appliances, but leave on the lights on.

Answer:
B

Scenario Question 9

But what if the odor is only faint? If Elisabeth realizes that the smell is not strong, then she knows there is no need to leave the house or call for help. Is this true or false?

    A. True
    B. False

Answer:
B

Scenario Question 10

When the odor is faint, there are still certain things to be done. What steps should Elisabeth take to ensure the safety of herself and her family? Put the steps in the correct order.

____Call the utility company and emergency responders.
____Leave the house.
____Open all doors and windows.
____Gather family members and pets.
____Shut off the gas supply, if she knows how.

Answer:
5, 4, 1, 3, 2

Preventing a Leak

Whether the gas odor is strong or faint, there are things Elisabeth can do to prevent a gas leak and keep her family safe.

There is no device that will detect a natural gas leak. So you should always be aware of the signs of a gas leak you have learned. By doing so, you can prevent gas leaks from harming your family.

There are devices that will alert you to another risk: carbon monoxide (CO) poisoning.

CO is produced by the incomplete burning of solid, liquid, and gaseous fuels. CO is colorless, tasteless, and odorless. You can install a carbon monoxide detector that will let you know if you are at risk of CO poisoning.

Scenario Question 11

While her parents are working downstairs, Claire is upstairs getting ready to clean the bathroom. What three things should she do first?

A. Turn on fan.
B. Open all cleaning supplies.
C. Put on gloves.
D. Read product labels.

Answer:
A, C, D

Scenario Question 12

Claire is in the middle of cleaning when she realizes she's almost out of toilet bowl cleaner. She has a full container of the cleaning chemical she uses on the bathtub. She decides just to mix the remaining toilet bowl cleaner with some of the bathtub cleaner. Which of the following would you advise Claire to do?

A. She should mix the two products only if it will create a stronger product.
B. Since the bathtub cleaner contains less than 5% ammonia, according to the label, she can mix it with anything.
C. As long as there is ventilation, she is safe to mix the products.
D. She should avoid mixing cleaning products.

Answer:
D

Scenario Question 13

Oh no! If there is an accident and Claire gets any of the chemical in her eyes, what should she do?

    A. Call 911 and wait for help.
    B. Wait 10 minutes to see about possible reaction and then flush with water.
    C. Flush with water for at least 15 minutes.
    D. Blot eyes with a paper towel to remove cleaner and then flush with water.

Answer:
C

Scenario Question 14

If Claire wants to avoid getting a headache from the fumes, what could she do?

    A. Spray air freshener to dispel any fumes.
    B. Since the label says the fumes are odorless, she doesn't have to worry about fumes affecting her.
    C. Make sure she has proper ventilation, such as the fan or the window.

Answer:
C

Scenario Question 15

Claire checks her watch and realizes that it's almost time for her soccer practice. She looks around the room, and a few things catch her eye. Which of the following items could create a hazard if Claire doesn't deal with them before she leaves?

    A. A bucket of water sitting on the floor
    B. Dirty rags in the sink
    C. Empty container in the trash
    D. The ventilation fan
    E. An open container by the sink

Answer:
A, B, and E

Lesson Summary

In this lesson, you learned about actions that you can take to minimize hazardous material incidents.

Key points covered in this lesson include:

- Taking the time to read product labels can reduce the chances of an accident.
- In cases of a hazardous materials emergency, you need to evaluate the type of exposure and type of chemical involved before taking action.
- The NFPA placard system is an important way to identify fixed locations where hazardous materials are used or stored.
- The DOT placard system is an important way to recognize vehicles or containers that carry hazardous materials in transit.

You've completed this lesson. You're now ready to begin Lesson 3-3: Terrorism and CERT.

Module 3: Hazardous Materials and Terrorist Incidents
Lesson 3-3: Terrorism and CERT

Lesson Overview

Welcome to Lesson 3-3: Terrorism and CERT.

In this lesson, you'll learn about the many forms of terrorism and steps you can take to protect yourself and others.

After completing this lesson, you should be able to:

- Define *terrorism* and *weapons of mass destruction (WMD)*
- Identify actions you should take to prepare for and respond to a possible terrorist attack

It should take about **30 minutes** to complete this lesson.

Defining Terrorism and WMDs

Terrorism is defined as violence against civilians to further political or social objectives. Modern terrorist incidents often involve weapons of mass destruction (WMD). As you may recall from Lesson 3-1, all **weapons of mass destruction** are defined as hazardous materials.

You should be aware of these possible WMDs, and the steps needed to prepare for and protect yourself and your family from terrorist threats. Planning for a potential terrorist threat is actually a lot like planning for a natural disaster.

Terrorism preparedness requires you to:

- **Keep informed** about the terrorist threat and what you can do to protect yourself
- **Make a plan** that includes how you will communicate with family members
- **Assemble a disaster supply kit** that includes water and other items

Keeping Informed

Take the time to learn about the different types of WMDs. You need to understand the dangers because during a terrorist incident every second counts. Your life and the lives of your family may depend on knowing:

- The risks posed by the weapons that terrorists are most likely to use
- How to address each type of risk

The following pages provide more information about the types of terrorist threats and how you should respond.

Knowledge Review

Which of the following might be an example of a weapon of mass destruction (WMD)? Select all that apply. Remember, there are many different types of WMDs.

A. Sarin gas
B. Chlorine gas
C. Radioactive iodine
D. The Ebola virus
E. A nuclear blast
F. Agent Orange

Answer:
All of the above

Biological Threats

A biological terrorist attack involves the deliberate release of germs or other biological substances that will make people sick. There are many types of biological agents that could be used for this kind of attack, and not all of them cause contagious diseases.

Anthrax is one example of a noncontagious agent. The smallpox virus, however, is highly contagious and can be spread by person-to-person transmission. Every biological agent is spread in its own way. Some must be ingested, others are inhaled, and still others are absorbed through the skin.

Biological threats are sometimes very difficult to detect. The most likely way that a biological attack will be noticed is through an emerging pattern of unusual illness. Health care workers will report this pattern, and you will be informed through an emergency radio or television broadcast. If your community has established a special system, you may get a telephone call or a personal notice from emergency response workers.

The public officials who inform you of the attack may not be able to tell you immediately what to do to protect yourself. It takes time to determine exactly what sort of biological threat is present, how it should be treated, and who is most at risk.

So what should you do?

Protect Yourself!

In the event of a biological threat, you should watch the television, listen to the radio, or check the Internet for official news.

Remain alert for information about:

- Demographic: The area or demographic (specific groups) that authorities are concerned about.
- Disease Details: The signs or symptoms of the disease
- Medications or Vaccines: Whether they are being distributed, who should receive them, and where you can obtain them
- Post-Infection Care: Where you can seek emergency medical care if you become sick

If you become aware of an unusual or suspicious release of an unknown substance nearby, don't waste time — protect yourself! Leave the area immediately. Use anything available to cover your mouth and nose with layers of fabric — a T-shirt, handkerchief, towel, or even tissue paper. These will help filter the air while still allowing you to breathe.

As soon as you can, wash yourself with soap and water and contact authorities to inform them of the incident.

Suspicions and Symptoms

If a family member falls ill during a declared biological emergency, it is important for you to keep a close eye on his or her symptoms. You should **not** automatically assume that his or her illness is a result of the biological attack.

Instead, seek medical advice and **pay attention to information provided by local public health or other government agencies.** Make sure to maintain good hygiene to avoid spreading germs.

Now let's discuss procedures for a chemical threat.

Chemical Threats

A chemical attack is the deliberate release of a toxic gas, liquid, or solid that can poison people and the environment.

Always be aware of your surroundings! You can detect the early signs of a chemical threat by remaining alert.

Possible signs of a chemical threat include:

- Many people suffering from watery eyes, twitching, choking, having trouble breathing, or losing coordination
- Several sick or dead birds, fish, or small animals

Protect Yourself!

If you do notice signs of a chemical attack, there are two things you should do:

1. You should quickly try to figure out exactly where the chemical is coming from and what the affected area is.
2. You should then immediately remove yourself from that area.

Exposure can take place indoors or outside. Safely exiting the area of the chemical threat depends on your location:

- If you are inside, attempt to leave the building without passing through the contaminated area. If this is not possible, remove yourself to the farthest possible location in the building and take shelter there. If you are outside, determine the fastest route to escape the chemical threat.
- If you are unable to leave the area, shelter in a location that is uphill and upwind from the threat.

In Case of Exposure

If your eyes are watering or your skin is stinging, and you are having trouble breathing, you may have been exposed to a chemical. After leaving the impacted area, you need to take the necessary precautions to minimize the danger:

- Remove everything, including jewelry
- Cut off any clothing that is usually removed over the head
- Wash your hands first, using any source of available cool water and soap
- Flush your entire body with cool water
- Blot yourself dry; do not rub

- Put on clean clothes if available
- Wait in safe area for professional responders to arrive

Knowledge Review

The following are statements concerning chemical and biological threats. Decide whether each statement is true or false.

1.   T   F   Biological threats can be difficult to detect.

2.   T   F   If you are exposed to a chemical threat, you should immediately scrub vourself with water.

3.   T   F   Biological agents are always extremely contagious.

4.   T   F   Several sick or dead fish may indicate a biological threat.

Answer:
   1. T
   2. F
   3. F
   4. T

Radiological Threats

A radiological threat is the use of common explosives to spread radioactive materials over a targeted area. Radiation threats are often referred to as "dirty bombs" or radiological dispersal devices (RDD). Radiation threats are **not** nuclear blasts; the force of the explosion and the radioactive contamination are much more localized.

The destruction left by the explosive will be immediately obvious to any observer, but radiation can be detected only by trained personnel using specialized equipment. While they define the presence of the radiation, you need to try to limit your exposure to it. Can you think of a few ways to do that?

Protect Yourself!

To limit the amount of radiation you are exposed to, there are three key things you need to consider: shielding, distance, and time.

1. Shielding: If you have a thick protective shield between yourself and the radioactive materials, more of the radiation will be absorbed, and you will be exposed to less.
2. Distance: The farther away you are from the blast and the fallout, the lower your exposure will be.
3. Time: Minimizing the time you are exposed will reduce your risk.

Nuclear Blast

A nuclear blast is an explosion that features intense light and heat, a damaging pressure wave, and widespread radioactive material that can contaminate the air, water, and ground surfaces for miles around.

Experts currently predict that a nuclear blast is less likely than other types of terrorist attacks. However, terrorism is by nature unpredictable, and it is good to be prepared for any potential emergency.

What would you do if a nuclear blast occurred?

Protect Yourself!

If there is the threat of a nuclear blast, **take cover immediately.** Go below ground, if possible, but any type of shield or shelter will help to protect you from the immediate effects of the blast and the pressure wave.

After the blast, try to assess the situation. Consider whether you can escape the area or if it would be better to take shelter in a nearby building. As we discussed earlier, you can protect yourself through shielding, distance, and time.

Knowledge Review

In the case of a radiological threat or nuclear blast, there are three concepts that will help you to limit the amount of radiation you are exposed to. Name and describe these three things.

____

____

____

Answer:
Three things you can do in case of a radiological threat or nuclear blast are:

- Shielding: If you have a thick protective shield between yourself and the radioactive materials, more of the radiation will be absorbed, and you will be exposed to less.
- Distance: The farther away you are from the blast and the fallout, the lower your exposure will be.
- Time: Minimizing the time you are exposed will reduce your risk.

Explosions

Explosions are another type of terrorist threat. If there is an explosion, quickly take shelter to shield yourself from the force of the blast as much as possible. Try bracing yourself against a sturdy desk or table. If you are inside, exit the building as soon as possible after the blast, because the structure may collapse.

When escaping the scene of the blast, you should:

- Locate your **emergency kit** if time allows
- Avoid elevators, because you may become trapped
- Check for fire and other hazards blocking exit routes

If there is a fire, what would you do?

In Case of Fire

Fire can complicate your escape route. A burning building presents many possible dangers. Do the following things to protect yourself:

- Crawl low if there is smoke in the air.
- Use a wet cloth to cover your nose and mouth.
- Use the back of your hand to feel closed doors. Feel the bottom, middle, and top of the door before opening it.

  o If the door is not hot, open it very slowly to avoid creating a vacuum for the fire.
  o If the door is hot, do NOT open it. Look for another way out.
- Use the stairs, never an elevator.
- Stop, drop, and roll if you catch fire.
- Never go back into a burning building.

Make a plan with family members in the event of a fire. As we will discuss later in this lesson, planning is an important part of safety. If a fire occurs while you are at home, account for all family members and carefully supervise small children.

Debris

An explosion in a building will generate a lot of falling debris. The structure of the building is weakened and can collapse easily — possibly on top of you.

If this happens and you're trapped by debris, there are some things you can do to protect yourself and help your rescuers find you. Don't yell for help unless it is absolutely necessary. Yelling will cause you to inhale a lot of dust and smoke. If possible:

- Signal Your Location: Use a flashlight or whistle to signal where you are.
- Avoid Unnecessary Movement: Moving excessively could kick up dust that will choke you.
- Make Noise: Tap on any pipes or walls that are within reach. Your rescuers will hear the sound.
- Breathe Through Filters: Cover your nose and mouth with anything available and breathe through the filter it creates.

Make a Plan

Your reaction during a terrorist incident depends a lot on where you are when it happens. Planning ahead will help you prepare for an attack anywhere, anytime. Plan for the possibility of a terrorist incident occurring while you're at home, at work, or on the road.

If you have kids in school, talk to them. Find out the school's emergency procedures, and make sure your kids know what to do in the case of a terrorist attack. They also need to know how to contact you and the rest of the family if something does happen. In other words, you need to make a family plan.

What do you think should be included in your family plan?

Your Family Plan

You and your family might not be together when a disaster strikes. Plan what to do and how to communicate during an emergency. Remember to
be patient. Telecommunications might be delayed or destroyed by the disaster, making it difficult to use the phone.

There are a few things to keep in mind while you plan:

- Long-Distance Contacts: Calling long distance may actually be easier than calling across town in the middle of a disaster. Find an out-of-state contact to act as a liaison among separated family members.
- Emergency Numbers: Make copies of all your emergency phone contacts and give them to all your family members.
- Means of Communication: If your family doesn't have cell phones, make sure everyone has a pre-paid phone card to call the emergency contact.

Emergency Information

Information is really important during and before a disaster. Find out what kind of disasters — both natural and manmade — are most likely to occur in your area. Find out how you will be informed of them, and where to get that information.

Different communities have different ways of spreading information, but most will use emergency broadcasts on the radio or television to get through to their citizens. Emergency alerts also sometimes include special sirens, door-to-door warnings, or individual telephone calls.

Call your local fire department, emergency management agency, or Red Cross chapter for emergency information that applies to your community.

Emergency Plans

Remember what we talked about earlier — your kids and their school's emergency plan? The same applies to daycare and other after-school activities, as well as your own work or office. Every location should have an emergency plan.

If none exists, volunteer to help create one. Talk to neighbors, co-workers, teachers, and daycare providers about how you can all work together in the event of an emergency. You'll be much better prepared to reunite with your family and loved ones if you plan ahead for a disaster.

Evacuate or Shelter in Place?

You never know whether you will need to evacuate or shelter in place during a terrorist attack. Anything could happen, so you must plan for everything. To find out what you should do, monitor the Emergency Alert System (EAS) broadcasts on local television channels or radio stations. Listen carefully and do exactly as you are directed.

Evacuate: *Evacuate only after assessing the situation outside! Do not evacuate if you see a lot of dust and debris.*

Shelter in Place: *Always shelter in place during a radioactive threat or nuclear blast.*

Knowledge Review

Different communities have different ways of spreading information. Who can you call to find out what sort of emergency information system your community uses?

A. The local television or radio station
B. The local Red Cross chapter
C. The local fire department or local emergency management agency
D. Your Neighborhood watch team chair

Answer:
B and C

Shelter in Place

To shelter in place, you need to:

- Bring your family and pets inside
- Close windows, air vents, and fireplace dampers; lock doors
- Turn off fans, air conditioning, and forced-air heating systems
- Take your emergency supply kit, unless you think it has been contaminated
- Go to an interior room with few or no windows
- Seal all windows, doors, and air vents in the interior room with plastic sheeting and duct tape
    - Measure and cut the sheeting in advance to save time
    - Be prepared to improvise and use what is on hand to seal gaps

Remember, sheltering in place is a **temporary** situation. It helps you survive temporary contamination. Listen to radio, television, and Internet news broadcasts, and stay put until local authorities advise that it is safe to leave your shelter.

Evacuate

When you are ordered to leave or decide that it is better to evacuate than to shelter in place, it helps to have an evacuation plan in mind. Plan where you'll assemble your family, and where you'll all go in case of a disaster. Make sure to choose many possible destinations so you have options.

To plan a successful evacuation:

- Plan meeting places for your family both inside and outside the neighborhood.
- Keep your car's gas tank half full at all times.
- Be familiar with alternate routes and methods of transportation out of your area.
- Be prepared to take your emergency supply kit with you.
- Always lock the door behind you.

Can you think of anything else that should be included in your plan?

Making a Plan

There are a few other things you can do when planning for or participating in a disaster evacuation.

Communicate
Communication is a very important part of your evacuation process.

- Call or e-mail the out-of-state contact in your family communications plan, and tell him or her where you are going.
- Leave a note inside your house telling others what time you left and where you are going.

Check to see if neighbors need a ride.

Turn Off Utilities
Knowing how and when to turn off utilities is also important.

- Remember: If you turn off the gas, a professional must turn it back on. Never attempt to do it by yourself.

- Locate the electric, gas, and water shutoff valves, and keep the necessary tools near gas and water shutoff valves.

Teach family members how to turn off utilities, and always turn off utilities if there is damage to your home or if authorities instruct you to.

Making a Plan for Pets

Pets need shelter, too. You shouldn't leave your pets behind when you're evacuating, but shelters usually are restricted to service animals. That means it's important to plan ahead and decide how your pets will be cared for in an emergency. Always store extra food, water, and supplies for your pet.

Make a Kit

We've already talked about making a supply kit for some of the disasters that may happen in your neighborhood. But the kit we prepared earlier doesn't have all of the supplies you need to get you through a terrorist incident.

In Module 1, Lesson 2, we discussed disaster supply kits. A good supply kit requires water, food, some basic supplies (such as whistles, flashlights and extra batteries, clothing, bedding, tools, a first aid kit, sanitation materials), and important family records (such as insurance policies and bank account information).

CERT and Terrorism

A terrorist attack is unlikely. However, it is always a possibility. If you observe something unusual or experience any of the symptoms that we discussed, terrorism might be to blame.

Do a complete assessment before you take any action. As we talked about earlier in the lesson, if a WMD has been used, even trained CERT members will be very limited in what they can do to help.

Remember that your own safety is your first priority!

Procedures

As we mentioned, there is very little CERTs can do to help during a WMD-related terrorist incident. Just as with hazardous materials, terrorist incidents should be a STOP sign for CERT members: WMD responses require special training and equipment.

That means that if you see any indications of a WMD, leave the area immediately and call emergency responders. Pay attention to the area as you leave it, because it is considered a crime scene. Report all your observations to the authorities.

Remember that you must never use a cell phone or two-way radio if you suspect that there is an explosive in the vicinity -- you could detonate it! Use a landline instead.

A Recap

Remember from earlier in the lesson that all WMDs are made of hazardous materials. If you think you have been exposed to chemical or radiological agents from a WMD, you need to take immediate action.

As we discussed in the Radiological Threat section and in Lesson 3-2: Hazardous Materials Safety, you must leave the area and use basic decontamination procedures to reduce your risk of injury and to limit your exposure to harmful substances.

Again, personal safety is your first priority. You should take self-protective measures only, and do not attempt to treat survivors in the contamination area. Instead, tell people to leave the area. Tell them how to do the basic decontamination procedure, and then tell them to wait for professional responders to perform complete decontamination.

Terrorist Incident Scenario

Natalie is at a train station in a mid-size American city with other commuters. They are all waiting for their trains. A man enters with a duffel bag, sets the bag on the ground, and walks away. As Natalie notices the bag, an announcement is made warning of a suspicious package.

Scenario Question 1

After noticing the bag and hearing the announcement, Natalie needs to take action. What should she do?

    A. Use a cell phone to call for help.
    B. Stay to help.
    C. Exit the station.

Answer:
C

Scenario Question 2

Let's say that Natalie is able to leave the station. Where should she go?
    A. She should go home and check on her family.
    B. She should get out of the station and move upwind and uphill.
    C. She should get out of the station but stay close.

Answer: B

Scenario Question 3

But what if Natalie didn't exit the station? By staying inside, she has put herself at risk of being trapped or harmed by an explosion or fire. If there were a fire, which of the following are appropriate actions to take?

    A. Attempt to extinguish the fire if it's small.
    B. Stay low to the ground if there's smoke.
    C. Use a wet cloth to cover your face.
    D. If the door is hot, brace yourself against it and open slowly.
    E. If you catch on fire, use the stop, drop, and roll method to put out the flames.
    F. Leave immediately, and don't return to the burning building.
    G. Use an elevator, as it can rise above the fire.

Answer:
B, C, E, and F

Scenario Question 4

In addition to fire, by staying in the station, Natalie also risks becoming trapped. It may become difficult to escape if you become trapped or injured amid debris. To avoid becoming trapped, assess the area around you and do not hurt yourself or others as you make your way through the affected area.

If you do become trapped, what is the best way to alert rescuers and others to your location in the rubble?

    A. Tap on a pipe or wall.
    B. Kick up dust in debris.
    C. Shout.
    D. Use a flashlight to signal.
    E. Use a whistle to signal.

Answer:
A, C, and E

Scenario Question 5

In addition to the risks of fire and becoming trapped, by remaining in the building Natalie is also at risk of an explosion.

Which of the following should you do if there is an explosion?

    A. Avoid using elevators.
    B. Stand in a doorframe for shelter.
    C. Immediately exit the building.
    D. Use a desk or table for shelter.
    E. Avoid escalators.
    F. Check for fire or other hazards.
    G. Don't use stairwells with windows.

Answer:
A, C, D, F

Scenario Question 6

It appears that the suspicious device also released a chemical agent. Which of the following could be signs of a chemical attack?

A. Irritation of eyes, skin, and throat
B. Sick or dead birds and other small animals
C. Difficulty breathing
D. Loss of coordination
E. Changes in skin color
F. Visible gas cloud
G. Cramps or diarrhea
H. Headaches, blurred vision, and dizziness

Answer:
All of the above

Scenario Question 7

If Natalie sees the signs of a chemical attack, what should she do first?
A. Help others.
B. Follow self-care procedures.
C. Identify impacted area and leave.

Answer:
C

Scenario Question 8

Once she is away from the impacted area, Natalie realizes she was still exposed to the chemical agent and begins to follow self-care procedures. In what order should the following self-care steps occur?

____Flush body with cool water
____Report to responders
____Remove clothing and jewelry
____Blot dry
____Cut off clothing instead of removing over heard
____Put on clean clothes
____Wash hands

Answer:
4, 7, 1, 5, 2, 6, 3

Scenario Question 9

Once she has left the station and the general area, Natalie shouldn't administer emergency care to those around her. But she should report the attack. What is the best procedure to follow when calling authorities in an emergency such as this?

   A. Since it's a terrorist attack, don't call 911. Immediately call the FBI or CIA.
   B. Call your family and have them call the authorities.
   C. Use a landline in a store or home to call 911.

Answer:
C

Scenario Question 10

Once Natalie calls 911, what should she tell them?

   A. Numbers and types of injuries
   B. What happened
   C. Observations she made about the culprit
   D. Where she is and how she can be reached
   E. What is happening now
   F. Where her family is
   G. The route authorities should take

Answer:
A, B, D, and E

Lesson Summary

This lesson discussed how to recognize and respond to terrorist incidents. You learned about the many forms of terrorism and steps you can take to protect yourself and others.

Key points covered in this lesson include:

- Personal safety is always your first priority.
- In the event of a terrorist attack, it is important to stay informed. Monitor television, radio, and Internet news broadcasts to keep on top of the situation.
- Always have a plan of action in case of terrorism. Your plan should include an emergency kit, an evacuation route, and supplies to shelter in place.

Module Summary

In Module 3: Hazardous Materials and Terrorist Incidents, you learned about two of the special situations that CERT members may encounter, and the ways that they protect themselves from the unique dangers presented by hazardous materials and terrorist incidents. These procedures are important for everyone to follow.

Key points included:

- Personal safety is always your first priority.
- Treat hazardous materials as STOP signs. Only professional responders with special equipment are trained to deal with these situations.
- If you become contaminated, use basic decontamination procedures and then wait for responders to perform complete decontamination.
- Taking the time to read product labels can reduce the chances of an accident.
- In cases of a hazardous materials emergency, you need to evaluate the type of exposure and type of chemical involved before taking action.
- The placard system is an important way to identify hazard levels.
- In the event of a terrorist attack, it is important to stay informed. Monitor television, radio, and Internet news broadcasts to keep on top of the situation.
- Always have a plan of action in case of terrorism. Your plan should include an emergency kit, an evacuation route, and supplies to shelter in place.

What's Next?

Now that you've completed this module, you're ready to move on to Module 4: Disaster Medical Operations. In that module, you'll learn how to recognize common injuries for which appropriately trained CERT members may provide basic care, and how to identify public health considerations at disaster sites. You'll also learn why dealing with disaster-related stress is important for both survivors and responders.

Module 4: Disaster Medical Operations
Lesson 4-1: Introduction to Disaster Medical Operations

Module Overview

Welcome to Module 4: Disaster Medical Operations.

This module will help you to prepare for the classroom *CERT Basic Training* course in disaster medical operations. There's a lot that CERT members can do to assist professional responders during a disaster, but some of the most exciting and challenging work has to do with disaster medical operations, where time is critical and every second counts.

In this module, you will get a preview of the CERT role in disaster medical operations and how CERTs identify and treat common injuries. These and other essential topics are covered in three separate lessons. It should take about 2 hours and 25 minutes to complete this module:

- Lesson 4-1: Introduction to Disaster Medical Operations — **15 minutes**
- Lesson 4-2: Principles and Guidelines for Survivor Care — **90 minutes**
- Lesson 4-3: Disaster Psychology — **40 minutes**

After completing this module, you should be able to:

- Identify the practices that CERTs must follow during disaster medical operations

Lesson Overview

Welcome to Lesson 4-1: Introduction to Disaster Medical Operations.

CERT members might have to act as first responders in a disaster until professional help is available. Survivors may need life-saving or life-sustaining treatment, and in this lesson you will learn how CERTs are able to help. **Note:** You should **not** apply the medical treatment skills discussed in this lesson until you have learned how to perform them by completing the classroom training!

The other lessons in Module 4 will build on this foundation. A good understanding of these fundamentals will be helpful when you take the *CERT Basic Training* course in disaster medical operations.

After completing this lesson you should be able to:

- State the role of CERTs in disaster medical operations
- Identify safety precautions for medical operations workers

It should take about 15 minutes to complete this lesson.

Planning for Disaster

Like everything else in disaster response, preparedness is key in planning
for medical operations. Therefore, CERT members should always assume that:

- Disasters often cause trauma-related injuries, and local medical resources
  may be overwhelmed or delayed in responding.
- Survivors of the incident will be the first source of help for the injured and
  will need to know what to do to help.

Because professional responders may be delayed in getting to the scene, CERTs
will need to be able to provide immediate care for life-threatening injuries.

What do you think "immediate care" might involve?

What CERTs Can Do

As a trained CERT member, you can provide help where it's needed most by
conducting triage, by providing immediate care and life-saving and life-sustaining
treatment, by performing head-to-toe assessments, by establishing medical
treatment areas, and by managing disaster-related stress in yourself and in other
survivors that you encounter.

CERT members can help where it's most needed by:

- Conducting triage
- Performing head-to-toe assessments
- Providing immediate care through life-saving and life-sustaining assistance
- Organizing medical treatment areas
- Helping to manage disaster-related stress felt by all survivors

CERT members are not alone in these tasks. They always work side by side with a
partner, or "buddy." The CERT member and his or her buddy will support,
encourage, and protect each other during disaster medical operations.

As this lesson continues, you will learn more about how CERT members protect
themselves and their buddies while carrying out the role of first responder.

Triage: *Process of sorting survivors according to the severity of their condition.*

Knowledge Review

A CERT activates in response to a tornado that dealt major damage to the neighborhood. What should CERT members assume as they prepare to deal with the medical needs of the survivors ?

    A. Disasters often cause trauma-related injuries.
    B. Local medical resources may be overwhelmed or delayed in responding.
    C. CERT members must wait for professional responders before dealing with any life-threatening injuries.
    D. Survivors of the incident will be the first source of help for the injured and need to know what to do to help.

Answer:
All of the above

Speed Is Essential

One of the most challenging things about disaster medical assistance is the time constraint. It is important to be able to quickly size up injuries and understand their relative severity, because every second may mean the difference between life and death! CERT members have to prioritize survivors' needs and adjust their own efforts accordingly.

Remember from earlier lessons that CERT members must complete a size up before taking action. This requires them to:

1. Gather facts
2. Assess and communicate the damage
3. Consider probabilities
4. Assess his or her own situation
5. Establish priorities
6. Make decisions
7. Develop plans of action
8. Take action
9. Evaluate progress

Time **can** be on a CERT's side: Neighborhood and workplace teams are often able to respond more quickly to immediate needs than professional responders are.

However...

The CERT Role

... Once professional responders do arrive, CERT members become secondary and must take direction from professionals if asked to assist.

The CERT Basic Training course will prepare you to help disaster survivors, and teach you skills that may save lives.

The CERT Goal

A CERT member's **goal** is to act safely to do the greatest good for the greatest number of survivors. This requires CERT members to:

- Size up the situation to determine if it is safe to act.
- Triage survivors quickly, identifying those with the most serious injuries.
- Treat those with the most serious injuries first.

Knowledge Review

After a disaster, when CERT members respond to survivors in their immediate area before professional responders arrive, their first priority will be to:

A. Triage survivors and treat those with life-threatening conditions
B. Organize disaster treatment areas
C. Make sure they are wearing the appropriate safety equipment
D. Keep onlookers away from the survivors

Answer:
C

Safety Equipment

All qualified CERT members use basic safety equipment called personal protective equipment (PPE). This includes work gloves, goggles, an N95 filter mask, a safety helmet, and sturdy shoes or boots.

In addition to this equipment, CERT members need to take special precautions when performing disaster medical operations. These measures protect them from blood-borne pathogens and other medical hazards.

Safety is the first step a CERT member takes — it comes before setting up a medical response area, before conducting triage, and before beginning preliminary treatment.

In addition to standard CERT PPE, non-latex exam gloves are also needed when providing medical assistance. When you're working with a survivor, **always** wear non-latex gloves, goggles, and a mask. Remember to always change or disinfect your non-latex gloves between survivors.

You'll learn more on how to change and sterilize gloves during the classroom-based *CERT Basic Training* course.

Knowledge Review

Safety is of the utmost importance at a disaster site. Select the items that a CERT member should use as safety precautions during disaster medical operations.

    A. Plastic sheeting
    B. Non-latex gloves
    C. Duct tape
    D. Masks
    E. Sterile hypodermic needles
    F. Hydrogen peroxide
    G. Goggles

Answer:
B, D, G

Keep Your Distance

Stop! Protect yourself. If there is evidence of chemical materials, do not approach.

In earlier lessons, you learned about avoiding dangerous situations such as hazardous materials and terrorist attack sites. In other words, another important part of protecting yourself is knowing when to stay away. There are also some medical situations that you should avoid.

Medical disasters caused by radioactive and chemical threats serve as stop signs for CERT members. Even with CERT PPE, these situations are dangerous. Rather than attempting to help on their own, CERT members should leave the area to avoid endangering themselves or spreading contamination.

Remember that only trained professionals with specialized equipment should respond to these medical disaster situations.

Death From Trauma

Medically, "trauma" refers to a serious or critical bodily injury or shock. Disasters often cause trauma-related injuries, but they can cause minor injuries, too.

Disaster trauma victims who die from their injuries can be divided into three categories according to their risk of death. Understanding these three phases can help CERT members use their training effectively, so that they can provide the best possible amount of assistance to survivors.

Phases of death:

1. Those who will die within minutes as a result of overwhelming and irreversible damage to vital organs
2. Those who will die within several hours due to excessive bleeding
3. Those who will die within several days or weeks from infection or multiple-organ failure (i.e., complications of the injury)

Research shows that more than 40% of people in phases 2 and 3 can be saved by providing simple medical care — care that **you** will soon be able to give them. **You** can prevent death from disaster trauma!

Knowledge Review

Disaster trauma victims who die from their injuries can be divided into three categories. Briefly identify these categories. Write your answers below and compare to the answers given.

____

____

____

____

____

Answer:
1. Those who will die within minutes as a result of overwhelming and irreversible damage to vital organs
2. Those who will die within several hours due to excessive bleeding
3. Those who will die within several days or weeks from infection or multiple organ failure (i.e., complications of the injury)

Lesson Summary

This lesson discussed disaster medical operations for CERTs.

Key points covered in this lesson include:

- The CERT goal is to stay safe and do the greatest good for the greatest number of survivors.
- Trauma injuries in disasters can often result in death. Sometimes these deaths can be prevented through simple, early treatment. CERT members are trained to provide this treatment until medical professionals are available to help.
- Do not apply the medical treatment skills covered in this module until you have completed classroom *CERT Basic Training* course.

You've completed this lesson. You're now ready to begin Lesson 4-2: Principles and Guidelines for Survivor Care.

Module 4: Disaster Medical Operations
Lesson 4-2: Principles and Guidelines for Survivor Care

Lesson Overview

Welcome to Lesson 4-2: Principles and Guidelines for Survivor Care.

In this lesson, you'll learn to identify key principles and practices for the medical care of disaster survivors.

After completing this lesson you should be able to:

- Identify signs of an obstructed airway, excessive bleeding, and shock
- State the steps to follow to open an airway, control bleeding, and treat for shock
- Define *triage* and its purpose in disaster medical operations
- Explain why it is important to follow procedures for head-to-toe patient assessment
- Identify common injuries for which appropriately trained CERT members may provide basic care as part of disaster medical operations
- Identify factors that are considered when establishing medical treatment areas
- Identify public health measures required at a disaster site

It should take you about **90** minutes to complete this lesson.

Life-Threatening Conditions

There are three life-threatening conditions that always get first priority when you're treating survivors. The conditions are often referred to as the "killers," implying that any time a survivor has one of these conditions, he or she will require immediate attention.

The killers are:

- Obstructed airway
- Excessive bleeding
- Shock

This lesson will introduce opening the airway, controlling excessive bleeding, and recognizing shock.

Protect Yourself!

Before we start, remember: Always protect yourself. When you perform disaster medical operations, remember to:

- Work with a buddy
- Do a good sizeup
- Wear safety equipment such as gloves, goggles, mask, helmet, and boots
- Wear non-latex gloves
- Change or sterilize gloves between patients
- Avoid high-risk situations, such as hazardous materials

Obstructed Airway

The first "killer" is an obstructed airway. The tongue is the most common airway obstruction. If the survivor is unconscious or semiconscious, the tongue may relax and block the airway, especially if the survivor is lying on his or her back.

Immediately attend to a person if he or she doesn't appear to be breathing. If you suspect the airway is obstructed, you'll need to attempt to open the airway to restore breathing.

Opening the Airway

To open the airway of a person who appears to be unconscious, **look**, **listen**, and **feel** for air exchange. The proper steps are:

1. Shake the person and shout: Can you hear me?
2. If the person doesn't respond, place your palm on his or her forehead.
3. Place two fingers of the other hand under the person's chin and lift the jaw while tilting the head back slightly.
4. Place your ear over the person's mouth and your hand on the person's stomach and look at the person's chest.
5. Look for chest rise.
6. Listen for breathing.
7. Feel for abdominal movement.

Maintaining the Airway

Make one or two attempts to open the airway. If breathing is restored, the airway must be maintained in an open position with the head tilt. You have several options for maintaining an open airway.

- You can have a volunteer hold the head in place.
- Or you can place soft objects under the person's shoulders to slightly elevate the shoulders and keep the airway open.

In the classroom *CERT Basic Training* course, you will learn more about these practices. You'll also learn to use them as they should be conducted in a disaster setting.

Knowledge Review

What is the most common airway obstruction in an unconscious or semiconscious person?

A. Vomit
B. Blood
C. Tongue
D. A small object

Answer:
C

Excessive Bleeding

The second "killer" is excessive bleeding. If not controlled, excessive bleeding can cause weakness, shock, or death.

Uncontrolled bleeding first causes weakness. If the uncontrolled bleeding continues, the person will go into shock within a short period of time. Death may then occur if a person loses just one liter of blood. (An adult has about five liters of blood.)

Types of Bleeding

There are three types of bleeding, depending on the type of vessel that is injured. The type of bleeding can usually be identified by how the blood flows. There are three types:

Arterial
Spurting: Arteries transport blood under high pressure. Bleeding from an artery is bright red blood that spurts with every heartbeat.

Venous
Steady flow: Veins carry blood under low pressure. Bleeding from a vein is a steady flow of darker blood.

Capillary
Oozing: Capillaries also carry blood under low pressure. Bleeding from capillaries oozes.

Controlling Bleeding

There are three main methods you should use to control bleeding:

- Direct pressure on the wound
- Elevation
- Pressure points

Don't use these steps until you complete the *CERT Basic Training* classroom training. But let's take a look at each to give you a brief introduction.

Using Direct Pressure to Control Bleeding

You can use these three steps to control bleeding using direct pressure:

1. Put a clean dressing over the wound and press firmly.
2. Use a pressure bandage to maintain pressure on the dressing.
3. Tie the ends of the bandage over the wound with a bow instead of a knot. The bow allows the bandage to be loosened later to reduce the pressure if the extremity becomes numb or turns blue. A bow also allows the wound to be checked for infection. Then, the bandage can be retied, saving time and supplies.

Dressing: *A dressing is applied directly to a wound; a bandage holds the dressing in place.*

Using Elevation to Control Bleeding

You can use elevation in combination with direct pressure to control bleeding. To use this method:

- First, elevate the wound above the level of the heart. This helps stop the bleeding.

- Then, try to find a position that the survivor can maintain with comfort. If necessary, you can prop the limb up with nearby objects.

It can take 5 to 7 minutes to completely stop the bleeding when using both direct pressure and elevation. Using a dressing and pressure bandage to maintain the pressure on the wound allows you to move on to the next survivor.

Using Pressure Points to Control Arterial Bleeding

A pressure point is where a major artery to an arm or leg crosses over a bone. When you press firmly on a pressure point, you can slow or stop the flow of blood to the bleeding arm or leg.

The pressure points labeled in the diagram are the brachial points for the arms and the femoral points for the legs.

Knowledge Review

At a disaster scene, you have discovered a barely conscious survivor bleeding profusely from a gash just above the knee. Blood is spurting rhythmically from the wound.

What methods could you use to control bleeding?

A. Put direct pressure on the wound.
B. Elevate the heart above the wound.
C. Elevate the wound above the heart.
D. Press on the brachial pressure point.
E. If still bleeding after 5 to 7 minutes, apply pressure to the femoral pressure point for that leg.

Answer:
A, C, and E

Shock

The third "killer" is shock, a disorder resulting from ineffective circulation of blood. If a survivor remains in shock, it can lead to the death of cells, tissues, and entire organs.

The body can compensate for blood loss or poor circulation and initially may mask the symptoms of shock.

It's very important that you evaluate patients for shock and monitor their conditions continually.

Signs of Shock

How do I know if someone is in shock?

Recognizing Shock

A survivor may display one or more signs of shock. There are several shock symptoms you should be able to identify. They include:

- Rapid, shallow breathing
- Capillary refill of greater than two seconds
- Failure to respond to a simple command, such as "Squeeze my hand"

Let's take a look at each of these symptoms.

Signs of Shock

There are three different signs of shock:

1. Slow Capillary Refill: A person experiencing shock may have slow capillary refill. This means the capillaries take longer than two seconds to refill and return the skin to normal color. Methods to check for capillary refill will be covered in the classroom training.
2. Rapid Breathing: A survivor whose breathing is rapid and shallow could be in shock. The person's breathing will sound like panting and will be more than 30 breaths per minute.
3. Failure to Respond: The survivor may fail to follow simple commands. Shock can make a traumatized person appear restless, nervous, or agitated, confused or dazed, or unaware of his or her surroundings. Try holding the person's hand and giving a simple command, such as: Squeeze my hand.

Knowledge Review

Which of the following statements are true about shock?

A. Shock results from the ineffective circulation of blood.
B. Remaining in shock can lead to the death of cells, tissues, and organs.
C. Slow, steady breathing is one sign of shock.
D. In most cases, the signs of shock are immediately apparent.
E. Survivor may seem dazed or confused.

Answer:
A, B, E

Triage

Your understanding of how to identify the three "killers" will be critical when you conduct triage.

Triage is the process of sorting survivors according to the severity of their condition. Your goal in triage is to identify survivors who are having problems with the three "killers" and treat them immediately.

You usually begin triage at the incident site, as soon as survivors are located. Evaluate survivors for airway problems, excessive bleeding, and shock. Sort by those who need immediate treatment and those who can wait until others have been triaged.

Why and when should you use triage?

Benefits of Triage

You should use triage in situations where resources or time may be limited. Triage was initially created for use in the military. The military's experience has shown the process to be especially effective in situations where:

- There are more survivors than rescuers
- There are limited resources
- Time is critical

This makes triage especially helpful for situations that CERTs may face.

Triage Categories

During triage, you will evaluate the conditions of survivors and victims and sort them into four categories:

- Immediate (I) - Survivor has life-threatening injuries (airway, bleeding, or shock) that demand immediate attention to save the person's life.
- Delayed (D) - Injuries don't jeopardize the survivor's life. The survivor may need care, but it can be delayed while triaging other survivors.
- Minor (M) –Survivor has insignificant injury (e.g., minor abrasion on a knee.) The survivor may need minor care, and might also assist rescuers in helping others with more serious injuries.
- Dead - Not breathing after two attempts to open the airway. There isn't time or resources to do CPR if others need immediate help.

All survivors and victims get identified or triaged with one of these categories to identify them. During your classroom training, you may learn a different tagging system used in your area.

Triage Precautions

Use caution when conducting triage! You should always be aware of your and your buddy's welfare as you take care of survivors. If you don't protect yourself, you can make the situation worse.

There are several precautions to take as you conduct triage, including:

- Avoiding hazardous materials
- Avoiding unsafe situations
- Wearing your safety equipment
- Wearing sterile gloves when treating survivors
- Changing or sterilizing gloves between survivors

You can also protect yourself with safety equipment, including goggles, dust mask, helmet, and sturdy shoes or boots. For gloves, a supply of exam gloves works best. If possible, when conducting triage, you should change exam gloves between survivors to avoid cross-contamination.

Conducting a Triage Evaluation

Recognizing the three "killers" was introduced earlier in the lesson. Triage involves three steps for checking for the "killers":

1. Check airway and breathing.
2. Check bleeding and circulation.

3. Check mental status.

Following these steps will help you triage survivors. And, in order to identify and treat life-threatening injuries as quickly as possible when there are multiple survivors, CERT members must follow specific triage protocols.

In short, protocols are:

- If the survivor fails the test for one of the three "killers," the status is "I."
- If the survivor passes all tests, he or she can wait for delayed treatment, and the status is "D."
- Everyone gets identified or triaged.

Remember, all "I's" get airway management, bleeding control, and treatment for shock before you and your buddy move to the next survivor.

You will learn and practice triage protocols in the classroom training. Don't try these procedures until you have received classroom training!

Knowledge Review

The goal of triage is to:

A. Decide which CERT members will treat which survivors.
B. Make sure that the workload is spread evenly among the rescuers.
C. Ensure an even flow of survivors to the patient treatment areas.
D. Identify and treat survivors who are "Immediates" as rapidly as possible.

Answer:
D

Patient Assessment and Treatment

Not all survivors will have life-threatening injuries. Many will have less critical injuries requiring basic care.

Common injuries that may require initial treatment by CERT members during a disaster include:

- Burns
- Wounds
- Fractures, sprains, and strains
- Hypothermia

You can determine injuries by conducting a head-to-toe assessment.

What Is a Head-to-Toe Assessment?

After all survivors in the area have been through triage, you can begin head-to-toe survivor assessments.

Head-to-toe assessment allows you to determine, as clearly as possible, the extent of injuries. Then, you can determine what type of treatment is needed and document any injuries.

Be sure that you assess all survivors! Injuries are not always immediately apparent; those who appear unhurt may be suffering, too.

What Are You Looking For?

During an assessment, you will look for indicators that help you determine the nature of the person's injury. Indicators may include bruising, swelling, and pain.

You should also try to find the "mechanism of injury." This is how a person has been hurt and may point to probable injuries.

Your assessment can be both hands-on and verbal.

Talk to the Survivor!

If the survivor is conscious, your assessment should be both hands-on and verbal. There are several important reasons to talk to the survivor during assessment.

First, you need **to ask permission**. The survivor has the right to refuse your help. You should always ask permission before you conduct the assessment.

Then, you should talk **to calm the person**. Tell the person who you are and what you are doing, to help reduce his or her anxiety.

Finally, **to obtain information,** you can ask questions. Ask the person to describe his or her symptoms and to tell you how the injury occurred.

Assessment Guidelines

There are several things you should keep in mind as you conduct a head-to-toe assessment. Follow these guidelines:

Be alert. Pay careful attention, using all of your senses. Look, listen, and feel for anything unusual.

Be thorough. Perform an entire assessment before beginning any treatment.

Be cautious. Treat all unconscious survivors as if they have a spinal injury.

Be consistent. Conduct assessments systematically, the same way every time.

Knowledge Review

Should the following tasks be part of a head-to-toe assessment of a conscious survivor? Select Yes or No for each task.

1.	Y	N	Ask permission to conduct an assessment.
2.	Y	N	Explain what you are doing.
3.	Y	N	Assess the type and extent of injuries.
4.	Y	N	Identify the mechanism of injury.
5.	Y	N	Determine what kind of treatment is needed.
6.	Y	N	Provide treatment for identified injuries as you find them.
7.	Y	N	Document injuries.

Answer:
1. Y
2. Y
3. Y
4. Y
5. Y
6. N
7. Y

Identifying Neck, Spine, and Head Injuries

Stop!

Before you go any further, you must check for neck, spine, and head injuries. A neck, spine, or closed-head injury is extremely serious. This type of injury must be identified immediately so that important precautions can be taken.

Common signs of a neck, spine, or closed-head injury are:

- Change in consciousness
- Inability to move one or more body parts
- Severe pain or pressure in the head, neck, or back
- Tingling or numbness in extremities
- Difficulty breathing or seeing
- Heavy bleeding, bruising, or deformity of the head or spine
- Blood or fluid in the nose or ears
- Bruising behind the ear
- Raccoon eyes (bruising around the eyes)
- Uneven pupils
- Seizures
- Nausea or vomiting
- Mechanism of injury that could cause this type of injury, such as when a survivor is found under collapsed building material.

A survivor who exhibits any of these signs should be handled so as to avoid further injury.

Handling Neck, Spine, and Head Injuries

If someone has a neck, spine, or head injury, your main goal is to do no harm. To avoid further injury, keep the head, neck, and spine in a straight line during the assessment. This is called "in-line stabilization." Continue to keep it straight as you treat other life-threatening injuries.

You'll learn the technique and practice in-line stabilization in the classroom training.

Knowledge Review

The primary objective of treating a spinal or neck injury is to:

A. Prevent further injury by keeping the spine in a straight line.
B. Determine the extent of the injury.

C. Move the survivor as quickly as possible to a treatment area.
D. Do nothing and wait for professional responders.

Answer:
A

Basic Care for Common Injuries

During your patient assessment, you may notice a wide variety of injuries. There are treatments you can learn for the following injuries:

- Burns
- Wounds
- Fractures, sprains, and strains
- Hypothermia

Basic information in this lesson will help you become familiar with the injuries and recommended treatments. **But remember, don't try to apply these treatments until you have had classroom training!**

Burns

Burns may be caused by heat, chemicals, electrical current, or radiation. The severity of a burn depends on:

- The temperature of the burning agent
- How long the survivor was exposed
- Area of the body affected
- Size of the burned area
- Depth of the burn

Always use extreme caution around burn survivors when there is no obvious cause for the burns. If the burns were caused by chemicals or radiation, you may be at risk.

Recognizing Burn Severity

The skin has three layers. Burns may affect one, two, or all three layers of skin.

The **epidermis** is the outer layer of skin. It contains nerve endings and is penetrated by hairs.

The **dermis** is the middle layer of skin. It contains blood vessels, oil glands, hair follicles, and sweat glands.

The **subcutaneous layer** is the innermost layer of skin, also called the hypodermis. It contains blood vessels and fat and overlies the muscle.

Skin layers are used to determine burn classifications.

Burn Classifications

Burns are classified into three degrees of severity, depending on the skin layers affected by the burn. The three categories are superficial, partial thickness, and full thickness.

Superficial burn

Skin layer:

- Epidermis

Symptoms:

- Reddened, dry skin
- Pain
- Possible swelling

Partial thickness burn

Skin layer:

- Epidermis
- Partial destruction of dermis

Symptoms

- Reddened, blistered skin
- Wet appearance
- Pain
- Possible swelling

Full thickness burn

Skin layer:

- Complete destruction of epidermis and dermis

- Possible subcutaneous damage

Symptoms:

- Whitened, leathery, or charred (brown or black)
- Painful or relatively painless

Treating Burns

You have three objectives when treating burns: cool the burn, avoid hypothermia, and cover to prevent infection.

Cool the Burn
Before you cool a burn you should first:

- Remove the survivor from the burn source and put out flames.
- Remove smoldering clothing unless stuck to the skin.

You should begin the process of cooling the burn. If the skin or clothing is still hot, you can cool it by immersing it in cool water for about 1 minute. Or you can apply cool compresses wrung out in cool water. You can use soaked towels, sheets, or other cloths. And do not forget -- make sure you remove heated metal objects from the survivor, such as watches and rings.

Avoiding Hypothermia
Be sure to use caution when you apply compresses. If you cool a burn too rapidly, you can cause hypothermia in some survivors. Those most likely to exhibit hypothermia include:

- Infants
- Young children
- Older persons
- People with severe burns

To avoid hypothermia in these survivors, do not cool more than 15 percent of the body surface area at one time. This should be about the size of one arm.

Covering
Cover the burn loosely with sterile dressings to keep air out and prevent infection. Follow your local protocols, which will determine whether dry or moist dressings should be used

Burn Treatment Do's and Don'ts

When you treat burns, remember these guidelines.

Do's

- Do elevate burned extremities higher than the heart.
- Do treat all survivors of third-degree burns for shock.

Don'ts

- Don't use ice. Ice causes vessel constriction.
- Don't apply antiseptics, ointments, or other remedies. Ointments hold heat in the burn area and will have to be scrubbed off later.
- Don't remove shreds of tissue or break blisters.
- Don't remove adhered particles of clothing. Instead, cut the clothing around the burn and leave the burned-in portion in place.

Knowledge Review

What treatments should you use on burns? Select Do or Don't for each statement.

1. Do   Don't   Remove smoldering clothing.

2. Do   Don't   Apply pain-relieving ointment to the burn.

3. Do   Don't   Immerse hot skin in cool water for up to 1 minute or apply cool compresses.

4. Do   Don't   Apply ice to the burn.

5. Do   Don't   Cool up to 50 percent of the body's surface at a time.

6. Do   Don't   Cover the burn with sterile dressings.

7. Do   Don't   Elevate burned extremities higher than the heart.

Answer:

1. Do
2. Don't
3. Do
4. Don't
5. Don't
6. Do
7. Do

Wounds

Wounds are common after disasters. Your objectives when treating a wound are to control bleeding and prevent secondary infection. You've already learned techniques to control bleeding. Now let's focus on preventing infection by cleaning and bandaging.

Wound Care: Cleaning

To clean dirt from a wound, follow this process:

- Irrigate the wound with water.
- Flush the wound with a mild soap-and-water solution.
- Irrigate the wound again with water.

In an emergency situation, you can use a bulb syringe — like a turkey baster — for irrigation.

Never scrub a wound!

Use sterile dressings and bandages to keep a wound clean after irrigating and to control bleeding.

Place a sterile dressing directly over the wound and secure it in place with a bandage. If the wound is still bleeding, use a pressure bandage to help control bleeding without interfering with circulation.

Wound Care Follow-up

Wound care follow-up depends on whether there is continued active bleeding.

If there is **no active bleeding**, remove the dressing, flush the wound, and check for signs of infection at least every four to six hours.

If there is **active bleeding** and the dressing is soaked with blood, redress over the existing dressing. Maintain pressure and elevation to control bleeding.

Be alert to an infection by noticing the signs. Signs of an infection include:

- Swelling around the wound site
- Discoloration
- Discharge from the wound
- Red striations from the wound site

Knowledge Review

After cleaning a wound and controlling bleeding, you should:

    A. Leave the wound to air-dry
    B. Apply an antibiotic spray, then bandage the wound.
    C. Apply a sterile dressing and clean bandage
    D. Apply ice to prevent future bleeding

Answer:
C

Fractures, Dislocations, Sprains, and Strains

In a disaster, survivors often sustain injuries to bones and joints, and to the muscles and ligaments that surround them.

There are several general treatment techniques that you can use on all four injuries:

- First, you should remove restrictive clothing, shoes, and jewelry that could act as tourniquets during swelling.
- Next, immobilize the injury and the joints immediately above and below the injury. We'll discuss this splinting method in a few screens.

Now let's look a little closer at the different injuries.

Fracture

Fractures are the first injury you should be aware of. There are four types of fractures:

- Closed fracture: Broken bone doesn't puncture the skin.
- Open fracture: Bone protrudes through the skin. With this type of injury, the wound allows contaminants to enter the fracture site.
- Displaced fracture: Bone is no longer aligned. If the limb is angled, there is a displaced fracture.
- Nondisplaced fracture: Bone remains aligned. A nondisplaced fracture can be hard to identify. The main signs are pain and swelling.

Treating Open Fractures

Open fractures are high-priority injuries because of the risk of severe bleeding and infection. Treat them quickly and check them frequently. Follow the Do's and Don'ts for treatment.

Do's

- Do cover the wound with a sterile dressing.
- Do splint the fracture without disturbing the wound.
- Do place a moist dressing over the bone end to keep it from drying out.

Don'ts

- Don't draw the exposed bone ends back into the tissue.
- Don't irrigate the wound.

Dislocations, Sprains, and Strains

You should also be aware of dislocations, sprains, and strains.

Dislocation
- Severe injury to the ligaments around a joint
- Bone separates from its normal position in the joint

Sprain
- Stretching or tearing of ligaments at a joint
- Usually caused by stretching or extending the joint beyond its normal limits
- Considered a partial dislocation
- Bone either remains in place or falls back into place after the injury

Strain
- Stretching and/or tearing of muscles or tendons
- Most often involves the muscles in the neck, back, thigh, or calf

Treating Dislocations, Sprains, and Strains

You may have difficulty identifying dislocations, sprains, and strains. The signs are often similar to those of a fracture. Symptoms may include:

- Tenderness at the site of the injury
- Swelling and/or bruising
- Restricted use or loss of use

Treat these injuries as fractures by immobilizing the injury.

Don't try to relocate a suspected dislocation!

Splinting

You can use splinting to immobilize an injured limb. Follow these basic guidelines for splinting:

1. Support the injured area above and below the site of the injury.
2. If possible, splint the injury in the position that you find it.
3. Don't try to realign bones.
4. Immobilize above and below the injury.
5. After splinting, check for proper circulation, including color, warmth, and sensation.

CERT classroom training will provide you with instruction and practice in splinting.

Knowledge Review

When treating an open fracture, which of the following treatments should be used?

A. Place a moist dressing over the bone end
B. Realign the bone ends, then apply a splint
C. Cover the wound with a sterile dressing
D. Irrigate the wound with soapy water
E. Splint the fracture without disturbing the wound
F. Draw the exposed bone ends back into the tissue

Answer:
A, C, and E

Hypothermia

Another injury you should look out for is hypothermia. Hypothermia occurs when the body's temperature drops below normal. It can occur in a matter of minutes.

Hypothermia is most often caused by:

- Exposure to cooler air or water

- Inadequate food combined with inadequate clothing and heat — especially in older people

What Are Signs of Hypothermia?

How can I tell if someone has hypothermia?

Symptoms of Hypothermia

You can tell if someone has hypothermia by looking at both primary and secondary signs and symptoms:

Primary:
- Body temperature of 95ºF (35ºC) or less
- Redness or blueness of the skin
- Numbness accompanied by shivering

Secondary:
- Slurred speech
- Unpredictable behavior
- Listlessness

Treating Hypothermia

You can treat survivors who are at risk for hypothermia by warming and protecting them. Follow these do's and don'ts:

Do's

- Do remove wet clothing and wrap the survivor in a blanket or sleeping bag that covers the head and neck.
- Do protect survivors from the weather.
- Do provide warm, sweet drinks and food if the survivor is conscious and coherent.
- Do place an unconscious survivor in the recovery position: on his or her side with knees drawn up.

Don'ts

- Don't attempt to warm the survivor by massaging arms or legs.
- Don't let survivors walk around, even if they seem fully recovered.
- Don't offer survivors alcohol.

Caution!

Remember that you haven't been trained to perform CERT functions. Proper CERT training requires classroom-based instruction and supervised practice!

Knowledge Review

Which of the following treatments are appropriate for a survivor with hypothermia?

A. Remove wet clothing
B. Massage extremities to increase blood flow
C. Wrap the survivor in a warm blanket
D. Encourage the survivor to walk around to speed circulation
E. Give the survivor cocoa and cookies if conscious and coherent
F. Offer the survivor warmed whiskey
G. Put the survivor in a place that is sheltered from the weather

Answer:
A, C, E, and G

Medical Treatment Area

Now that you've identified injuries, you need to have a place for survivors to wait for treatment, such as a medical treatment area.

Disaster medical operations are divided into four major components: triage, transport, treatment, and morgue.

Triage
The initial sorting of survivors based on the severity of their injuries. Triage begins wherever survivors are found, as part of search and rescue.

Transport
The movement of survivors from triage to the treatment area. If professional help will be delayed, CERT members may transport survivors to the treatment areas.

Treatment
Where survivors receive emergency medical services. It's divided into two areas: immediate care and delayed care.

Morgue
A temporary holding area for victims who have died.

Medical Treatment Areas

All four components are important. We've covered triage. Right now let's focus on medical treatment areas.

Organizational Issues

You can ensure that medical operations run efficiently during a disaster through organizational planning before a disaster occurs.

Your planning should address personnel assignments, provision of area markings, and documentation.

Begin with personnel.

Personnel Assignments

Personnel assignments are crucial to the effective operation of a CERT. To begin with, the CERT will assign leaders to maintain control in each of the medical treatment areas.

The treatment leader in each treatment area ensures orderly survivor placement. The leader then directs assistants in conducting patient assessments.

Area Markings

A clearly marked treatment area and morgue helps CERT members and professional responders efficiently treat survivors.

Prepare materials in advance so that they're available for immediate use. Materials include signs and, if possible, ground covers or tarps.

Use signs to identify areas for survivors and victims tagged "I," "D," "M," and "Dead." Ground covers or tarps can help to clearly mark the areas. Then volunteers will know exactly where to take survivors, and those marked "I" can immediately receive treatment.

If they're willing, survivors at the treatment area with minor injuries, tagged "M," may be able to assist trained CERT members.

You'll learn more about protocols and smart practices for setting up a CERT treatment area in the *CERT Basic Training* course.

Documentation

Thorough documentation of survivors and victims in the treatment areas and

morgue is a must. You should document the following information for each

person:

* Available identifying information
* Physical description -- age, sex, body build, estimated height
* Clothing
* Injuries
* Treatment
* Transfer location

This documentation then provides you with valuable sources of information for:

* Estimating the number of casualties by degree of severity
* Deploying resources effectively
* Tracking individual survivors and victims

The CERT classroom training provides additional information and forms for documenting survivors in the medical treatment area. You'll also learn about documenting other CERT operations and activities in the disaster setting.

Knowledge Review

It's the responsibility of medical treatment area leaders to:

A. Choose the best site for the medical treatment area
B. Oversee arrangement and assessment of survivors and victims
C. Conduct all patient evaluations
D. Manage the transport of survivors into the treatment areas

Answer:
B

Public Health Considerations

Public health becomes a concern when disaster survivors are grouped together for treatment

To protect the public health and avoid the spread of disease, you should:

* Maintain hygiene

- Maintain sanitation
- Use water purification (if necessary)

These are seemingly simple measures that can further protect lives when done properly.

Maintaining Hygiene

Proper hygiene is crucial wherever medical operations take place — even under makeshift conditions. There are a few important measures you can take to maintain hygiene.

Washing Hands

- Wash hands frequently.
- Use soap and water.
- Hand-washing should be thorough -- at least 12 to 15 seconds.
- Use an antibacterial scrub, if possible.
- Hand sanitizer can be used

Wearing sterile gloves

- Wear sterile gloves at all times.
- Change or disinfect gloves after examining and/or treating each patient.
- Under field conditions, you can use rubber gloves that are disinfected between survivors using diluted bleach of one part bleach to 10 parts water.

Wearing a mask and goggles

- Wear a mask. If possible, choose a dust mask that is rated N95. This type of mask will filter particles as small as 3 microns.
- Wear goggles to protect the eyes from splashed and airborne contaminants.

Using bandages and dressings

- Cover all open wounds to help prevent infection and the spread of disease.
- Keep bandages and dressings sterile.
- Don't remove the overwrap from bandages and dressings until you are ready to use them.
- After opening, use the entire bandage or dressing, if possible.

Staying away from body fluids

- Avoid contact with body fluids. Gloves, mask, and goggles provide an important barrier.

- If you come in contact with body fluids, thoroughly wash contaminated areas as soon as possible.
- Use soap and water or diluted bleach.

Maintaining Sanitation

Proper sanitation is a must in the medical treatment area. Proper sanitation helps prevent infection and the spread of disease.

To maintain sanitary conditions, medical personnel should:

- Put waste products, such as exam gloves and dressings, in plastic bags. Tie off the bags and label them "medical waste."
- Keep medical waste separate from other trash, and dispose of it as hazardous waste. CERTs follow local regulations for disposing of these waste products.
- Bury human waste.

Using Purified Water

As a rescuer, you shouldn't put anything on wounds other than purified water. The use of other solutions on wounds, such as hydrogen peroxide, must be the decision of trained medical personnel.

Because potable water supplies are often in short supply or unavailable in an extreme emergency, it may become necessary to purify water before using it.

Methods for Purifying Water

In a disaster situation, potable water may be unavailable. Therefore, always purify water for drinking, cooking, and medical use with one of the following methods.

Heat method

- Heat water to a rolling boil for 1 minute.

Water purification tablets

- Use iodine or chlorine tablets to kill waterborne pathogens. When using these tablets, follow the product directions provided.

Bleach

- Use unperfumed liquid bleach. Add 8 drops of bleach for each gallon of water. Mix well and let the bleach/water solution stand for 30 minutes.
- If the solution doesn't smell or taste of bleach, add another 8 drops of bleach and let the solution stand for 15 minutes before using.
- If the water is cloudy, double the recommended dosage of bleach.

Knowledge Review

There is heavy flooding in the wake of a hurricane. Widespread power outages have occurred, and the water supply has been contaminated.

Mark which techniques you can use to maintain hygiene when treating survivors.

1.   Yes   No   Wash or sanitize your hands frequently

2.   Yes   No   Wear exam gloves and change or disinfect them after each patient

3.   Yes   No   Wear a mask and goggles

4.   Yes   No   Avoid contact with body fluids

5.   Yes   No   Pour a water/bleach solution over all bandages before use

Answer:
   1. Y
   2. Y
   3. Y
   4. Y
   5. N

Remember!

Remember that you haven't been trained to perform CERT functions. Proper CERT training requires classroom-based instruction and supervised practice.

Don't try to use the procedures introduced in this lesson and course until you've completed the CERT classroom training.

Lesson Summary

This lesson discussed principles and guidelines for care of survivors by CERT members.

Key points covered in this lesson include:

- The three "killers" — obstructed airway, excessive bleeding, and shock
- Purpose of triage
- Purpose and importance of head-to-toe assessment
- Neck, spine, and head injuries
- Common injuries, such as burns and wounds
- The purpose of medical treatment areas
- Public health concerns after disasters

You've completed this lesson. You're now ready to begin Lesson 4-3: Disaster Psychology.

Module 4: Disaster Medical Operations
Lesson 4-3: Disaster Psychology

Lesson Overview

Welcome to Lesson 4-3: Disaster Psychology.

In this lesson, you'll learn about the actions that CERT members can take to deal with the psychological stresses that are associated with disaster response.

After completing this lesson you should be able to:

- State why dealing with disaster-related stress is important
- Identify steps you can take to relieve your own stressors, both individually and as part of a team
- Identify ways to help survivors with disaster trauma

It should take you about **40 minutes** to complete this lesson.

Coping With Disaster

During and after a disaster, both survivors and responders may experience situation-related stress. It's important for CERT members to understand the possible effects of these stressful events and how to cope with or lessen their effects.

In this lesson, you'll learn the steps that CERT members use to manage vicarious trauma.

Vicarious Trauma: *The emotional shift that can occur when CERT members interact closely with disaster survivors.*

The CERT Role

Disasters generate pain, suffering, loss, and grief on an enormous scale. CERT members have the role of stabilizing disaster scenes by stabilizing the individuals who have been affected.

But this job can be hard to do if CERT members are suffering their own personal stress from the disaster. This, together with the stress of vicarious trauma, can lessen CERT members' effectiveness during an emergency situation.

Can you think of any measures that CERT members should take to protect themselves from vicarious trauma?

Household construction level with air bubble in the middle, moving slightly left and right. Text reads: CERT members stabilize disaster situations by stabilizing the people who have been affected.

Protect Yourself!

There are three important measures that CERT members can take to protect themselves from the effects of vicarious trauma. These three measures can be divided into the "do's and don'ts" of disaster psychology.

Do

- Do be alert to signs of disaster trauma in yourself.
- Do take steps to reduce stress.

Don't

- Don't over-identify with other survivors. This increases your own stress.

Knowledge Review

What is a CERT member's primary psychological role in a disaster?

- A. Keep survivors from getting angry or depressed
- B. Stabilize the scene by stabilizing individuals
- C. Provide psychological counseling
- D. Convince survivors that their situation is better than it appears

Answer:
B

Don't Over-Identify

Let's break down the three ways that CERT members can protect themselves from psychological trauma during a disaster.

First, it is extremely important for CERT members to keep their emotional distance from other survivors. As CERT members work with and listen to disaster survivors, they'll probably have many of their own thoughts and feelings about the situation, creating added stressors.

If CERT members take on survivor feelings as their own, their stress level will increase and their level of effectiveness will decrease.

Recognize the Signs
Second, CERT members must carefully monitor themselves for signs of disaster-related trauma. By being alert to their reactions and state of mind, CERT members can help to alleviate their own stress.

Symptoms of stress can be **psychological, physical,** or **both.** Can you think of any examples?

The following types of psychological and physiological responses may be observed in survivors after a disaster:

Psychological symptoms

- Irritability or anger
- Self-blame or the blaming of others
- Isolation and withdrawal
- Fear of recurrence
- Feeling stunned, numb, or overwhelmed
- Feeling helpless
- Mood swings
- Sadness, depression, and grief
- Denial
- Concentration and memory problems
- Relationship conflicts and marital discord

Physiological symptoms

- Loss of appetite
- Headaches or chest pain
- Diarrhea, stomach pain, or nausea
- Hyperactivity
- Increase in alcohol or drug consumption
- Nightmares
- Inability to sleep
- Fatigue or low energy

Knowledge Review

Scott, a CERT member, responded to the disaster scene in his town after a devastating tornado. He spoke to many people who had lost their homes and possessions. Some people had lost family members. Gradually, Scott developed feelings of overwhelming sadness and hopelessness.

What are Scott's feelings an example of?

   A. Transference
   B. Stress
   C. Vicarious trauma
   D. Survivor trauma

Answer:
C

Reduce Stress

The **third** way that you can manage the effects of disaster trauma is to take preventive action to reduce stress.

Only **you** can determine what strategies work for you. If you identify your personal stress reducers before an incident occurs, you'll be better prepared to cope during disaster situations. A great way to practice reducing stress is by attending to the physical, emotional, psychological, and mental health needs in your daily life.

Slideshow animation: Bed representing sleep, food pyramid representing a balanced diet, bicycle representing exercise, and a red heart representing connection with others. Animation ends with all five and the words: All of these things help to reduce stress!

Stress Reducers

That's right! Stress reduction is something you can practice through daily activities.

Meet Your Physical Needs: Get enough sleep, exercise, and eat a balanced diet. Establish a moderate balance of work, pleasure, and downtime.

Meet Your Emotional Needs: Connect with others. Allow yourself to receive as well as give support.

Meet Your Psychological and Spiritual Needs: Use spiritual resources. If necessary, be willing to talk to mental health professionals.

Team Strategies

But how do CERT members cope with disaster-related stress?

CERT members can take advantage of their team to help them cope with the stress of disaster trauma. The CERT organization provides psychological support for all of its workers, and Team Leaders help members to establish **strategies** for dealing with stress.

The strategies fall into four main categories:

1. Training and communication
2. Teamwork
3. Pacing
4. Nutrition

Knowledge Review

Can you think of how a training and communication strategy can be used to reduce CERT member stress? Write your answers below and compare to the answers given.

____
____
____
____
____

Answer:

Training: Team Leaders encourage members to get stress management training.

Briefings: At the start of an incident, team leaders brief CERT personnel about the current situation and what they may see. This information helps dispel anxiety and helps team members prepare emotionally for the experience.

Teamwork Strategy

The Team Leader emphasizes the team aspects of CERT to remind members that they are not alone in their often difficult duties.

Team Focus: Working together and looking out for each other is an important method of combating stress.

Team Sharing: Team members should share not only the workload but also the emotional load. Team sharing helps to defuse pent-up emotions.

Pacing Strategies

Pacing strategies can also help CERT members deal with the stress of disaster work. Pacing strategies include breaks, rotation, and gradual phase-out.

Breaks allow rescuers to rest and regroup. Mental or physical fatigue reduces worker effectiveness and may result in unsafe acts, so it's important to encourage workers to take breaks **away** from the incident area to talk about their experiences.

Rotation allows members to move from high-stress to low-stress duties whenever possible, reducing the mental and physical strain of disaster work.

Gradual phase-out simply means that workers should be removed from the response effort gradually, and moved from high-stress to low-stress duties before leaving the scene.

The animation to the right suggests how CERT members cycle back and forth between low-stress and high-stress duties.

Nutrition Strategy

Finally, nutrition is an important strategy that CERT members use to cope with stress during a disaster. Teams use their rotated breaks to drink water and eat healthy foods, such as fruit and granola bars, avoiding excessive caffeine and refined sugar products in their snack choices.

As we discussed earlier, eating a healthy, balanced diet helps to reduce stress. On a disaster scene, it also helps to maintain alertness. Don't wait until you feel hungry or thirsty to take a break. If you feel thirsty, you're already dehydrated!

Knowledge Review

Amy is a Team Leader whose CERT has completed stress management training. Her team is activated and responds after a major earthquake. From experience, Amy knows that a high-magnitude earthquake causes a significant number of injuries and widespread damage and destruction.

As Team Leader, what can Amy do to reinforce her team's stress management training and provide psychological support for its members? Write your answers below and compare to the answers given.

____
____
____
____
____

Answer:

There are many strategies Amy can use as a CERT Team Leader to provide psychological support for her team members. She can:

- Brief members on what they can expect
- Emphasize team focus and encourage team sharing
- Create break times so that members can rest and regroup
- Rotate members away from the disaster scene during their breaks
- Gradually phase team members out of the response effort
- Ensure team member nutrition by telling them to drink water and allowing them to take meal breaks

Survivor Trauma

It's important for CERT members to understand potential survivor reactions. Anticipating certain reactions can help workers reduce their own stressors and improve their ability to respond effectively to the situation. We have already discussed a few possible psychological effects that disaster can have on both survivors and CERT workers.

But what about the emotional effects?

Emotional Phases

Survivors go through emotional phases when a disaster occurs. Four of these include:

- Impact Phase: Occurs at the time of the initial event. Survivors do not panic and may often show no emotion whatsoever.
- Inventory Phase: Immediately follows the event. Survivors assess damage and try to locate other survivors, usually searching for people who can help in rescue operations.
- Rescue Phase: Occurs when emergency services personnel — including CERTs — are responding. It is important for responders to identify themselves with helmets and vests, because survivors will take instructions from them without protest.
- Recovery Phase: Occurs when survivors begin to realize the reality of the situation. They begin to understand that their lives will never be the same, and they may become angry or react negatively toward their rescuers.

Knowledge Review

Disaster survivors go through distinct psychological phases. Place the phases in the correct order.

____Inventory Phase
____Recovery Phase
____Impact Phase
____Rescue Phase

Answer:
2, 4, 1, 3

Traumatic Stress

As we've discussed, survivors suffer from disasters on many levels. This is because **traumatic stress** is capable of affecting survivors in three major areas of their lives: cognitive functioning, physical health, and interpersonal relationships.

- Signs that a survivor's **cognitive functioning** has been affected appear when he or she acts irrationally or in ways that are out of character, or has difficulty making decisions and retrieving or sharing memories.
- **Physical** symptoms of traumatic stress may be chills, thirst, twitches, and muscle tremors, as well as fatigue, dizziness, weakness, and fainting. Nausea and headaches, elevated blood pressure, a rapid heart rate, and chest pain may also result.

- **Interpersonal relationships** may be affected because of a survivor's temporary or long-term personality changes.

Each person's reaction to a traumatic event will be different.

Traumatic Stress: *the emotional, cognitive, behavioral, physiological, and spiritual experience people have when they are exposed to or witness events that overwhelm their coping or problem-solving abilities.*

Mediating Factors

There are five mediating factors that may affect the strength and type of an individual's reaction to a traumatic event. These mediating factors include:

Prior experience with the same or similar event: The emotional effect of multiple events can be cumulative, leading to progressively greater stress reactions.

Intensity of the disruption in the survivor's life: The more the survivor's life is disrupted, the greater his or her psychological and physiological reactions may become.

Meaning of the event to the individual: The more catastrophic the survivor perceives the event to be, the more intense his or her stress reactions will be.

Elapsed time since the event: The reality of a traumatic event takes time to "sink in."

The fifth possible mediating factor is the **emotional well-being** of the survivor and the **type of resources** that he or she has for coping. People who have had other recent traumas may not cope well with additional stresses. Social resources are especially important coping mechanisms; people with fewer social connections or outlets may not cope as well as their well-connected peers.

As you can see, survivors often feature a range of responses. Survivor reaction varies from person to person, and the reactions CERT members see are part of the psychological impact of the event. A survivor's negative response may not relate to anything a CERT member has done.

Therefore CERT members should NOT take survivors' attitudes personally!

CERT Psychological Role

As we discussed earlier in the lesson, a CERT member's on-scene psychological role is to stabilize the disaster area by stabilizing individuals. There are four ways that CERT members go about this essential duty. They:

Step 1: **Assess** survivors for injury and shock

Step 2: **Involve** uninjured people in helping at the scene

Step 3: **Provide** support by listening and empathizing

Step 4: **Help** survivors connect to natural support systems

Disaster Psychology Scenario

It's a Wednesday morning inside a shopping center in a small city. A tornado touches down near the center, causing damage and injuring shoppers. Members from the local CERT Program arrive on the scene to help and set up a command post in the parking lot.

Scenario Question 1

The CERT members have arrived at the scene and are ready to work. But before they begin to assist survivors, they need to prepare. Which of the following are basic safety precautions the team should take?

    A. Avoid hazardous materials.
    B. Do nothing until professionals arrive.
    C. Avoid unsafe situations.
    D. Give their dust masks to survivors.
    E. Use proper personal protective equipment: helmet, goggles, mask, gloves, sturdy shoes or boots.

Answer:
A, C, and E

Scenario Question 2

Though they won't actually tag anyone, it's time for CERT members to conduct a triage evaluation. Two team members, Vince and Carly, begin to talk to survivors and gauge their injuries. First, they meet Bernadette and Lucy. What are the three "killers" Vince and Carly should look for in their evaluation?

    A. Shock
    B. Superficial bruises on head
    C. Obstructed airway
    D. Broken limb
    E. Dilated pupils
    F. Uncontrolled bleeding

Answer:
A, C, F

Scenario Question 3

Lucy has a headache but is alert. Other than a few bruises, she doesn't appear to have any other injuries. Bernadette has a bleeding head wound. She's also having trouble catching her breath. Based on what the CERT members observed, does Bernadette or Lucy require more immediate care?

    A. Bernadette
    B. Lucy

Answer:
A

Scenario Question 4

CERT member Carly is examining Lucy. Lucy insists that she is fine and just wants to go home. Since nothing is physically wrong with her, she thinks that she'll be fine and that she'll go home and forget about it. What are some effects of traumatic stress that Lucy might experience?

    A. Thirst
    B. Dizziness and fainting
    C. Difficulty making decisions
    D. Elevated blood pressure
    E. Muscle tremors
    F. Acting in ways that are out of character

Answer:
All

Scenario Question 5

Vince is still working with Bernadette. She is becoming increasingly distraught as Vince talks to her. Bernadette has a head injury but wants to get up and talk to others. She insists she must speak to her neighbor, whom she saw shopping before the tornado hit. Which of the emotional phases of a crisis is Bernadette likely experiencing?

    A. Impact
    B. Inventory
    C. Rescue
    D. Recover

Answer:
B

Scenario Question 6

Vince and Carly are still talking to Bernadette and Lucy. The psychological role of CERT in a disaster is to help stabilize the incident scene by stabilizing individuals. What should the CERT member do to stabilize the scene?

    A. Help survivors find their loved ones
    B. Remove survivors who are ready to leave the scene
    C. Assess the survivors for injury and shock
    D. Assist in any police investigation after all survivors have been helped
    E. Provide support by listening and empathizing
    F. Involve uninjured people in helping
    G. Help survivors connect to natural support systems

Answer:
C, E, F, G

Scenario Question 7

Sitting with Carly, Lucy begins to talk about herself. She's 21, has a younger brother at home, and is planning a trip with a friend next weekend. As she's talking, Carly can't help but think about her own daughter and young son. Her

daughter is the same age as Lucy, and they like the same kind of music. Now
Carly begins to worry about her own family. What could Carly be experiencing?

    A. Denial
    B. Transference
    C. Post-traumatic stress disorder
    D. Over-identification

Answer:
D

Scenario Question 8

Carly is becoming more upset and tells her team leader, Anna, she wants to
immediately leave and go home. Anna knows this isn't the best idea. What should
Anna have Carly do instead?

    A. Have a fellow team member drive her home
    B. Phase out
    C. Re-do CERT training

Answer:
B

Scenario Question 9

Javier is talking to Charlotte. Charlotte has a sprained ankle and a scratch on her
head but is mainly all right and seems in good spirits. However, team leader Anna
notices that Javier isn't doing so well. Javier is hyperactive and can't sit still. He
also says he's beginning to feel nauseous. Anna thinks these are physiological signs
of trauma. What are some psychological signs of stress that Javier might also be
experiencing?

    A. Isolation and withdrawal
    B. Fear of recurrence
    C. Feeling of invincibility
    D. Mood swings
    E. Self-blame
    F. Refusal to leave the scene

Answer:
A, B, D, and E

Scenario Question 10

Anna pulls Javier aside to talk. Javier tells her he's been working for several hours but insists he is fine to continue. Anna thinks he should take a break or rotate to another job. What should Anna tell Javier?

A. "I think you should sit down here with Charlotte and relax. Taking a break away from here will only make you more stressed that you aren't helping."
B. "You should go outside by yourself for a little while. Don't talk to other teammates, just relax."
C. "You should take a break. Get away from the damage and survivors for a bit and regroup. You don't want your exhaustion to affect your response efforts."
D. "Take a few minutes to walk around and see all the damage. That will help you understand the scope and inspire you to work harder."

Answer:
C

Scenario Question 11

Leslie was shopping for her dad's birthday gift when the tornado hit. She has a sprained ankle and a headache. Ramona has been talking to her, and other survivors, for most of the day. She's been careful to take breaks and talk to her teammates, but Anna still sees some signs of stress in her. She thinks that Ramona wasn't as mentally prepared for this disaster as she could have been. What advice should Anna give Ramona to help her deal with stress now and in the future?

A. Exercise.
B. Connect with others.
C. Eat a balanced diet.
D. Be willing to talk to mental health professionals.

Answer:
All

Lesson Summary

This lesson discussed how to identify actions that CERT members can take to deal with the psychological stresses that are associated with disaster response.

Key points covered in this lesson include:

- To limit the effects of vicarious trauma on yourself, don't over-identify with survivors. Monitor your own reactions and use stress reducers that work for you.
- Traumatic stress may affect a survivor's cognitive functioning, physical health, and interpersonal relationships.
- When working with survivors, the CERT psychological role is to stabilize the incident scene by stabilizing individuals.

Congratulations, you've completed this lesson.

Module Summary

In Module 4: Disaster Medical Operations, you learned that survivors of a disaster may need life-saving or life-sustaining treatment. You also learned how CERTs are able to help until professional responders arrive. We discussed the importance of disaster psychology, and we reviewed ways that you can cope with the stress of disaster situations.

Key points in this module included:

- The CERT goal is to stay safe and do the greatest good for the greatest number of survivors.
- Trauma injuries in disasters can often result in death. Sometimes these deaths can be prevented through simple, early treatment. CERT members are trained to provide this treatment until medical professionals are available to help.
- Do not apply the medical treatment skills covered in this module until you have completed classroom training.
- Medical conditions that always get priority are obstructed airway, excessive bleeding, and shock.
- The triage process is used to distinguish among those who need immediate care, those who can wait, and those who are dead.
- Clearly marked medical treatment areas and morgues help professional responders efficiently treat survivors.
- To limit the effects of vicarious trauma on yourself, don't over-identify with survivors. Monitor your own reactions and use stress reducers that work for you.
- Traumatic stress may affect a survivor's cognitive functioning, physical health, and interpersonal relationships.

- When working with survivors, the CERT psychological role is to stabilize the incident scene by stabilizing individuals.

What's Next?

Now that you've completed this module, you're ready to move on to Module 5: Search and Rescue. In that module, you'll learn about practices and techniques that CERTs use during search and rescue operations. Following these practices helps keep both rescuers and survivors safe in the wake of a disaster.

Module 5: Search and Rescue
Lesson 5-1: Introduction to Light Search and Rescue

Module Overview

When disaster strikes, everyone naturally wants to help the survivors. Unfortunately, untrained, spontaneous rescuers all too often end up becoming injured. CERT members, on the other hand, are prepared to respond to disasters safely and effectively. They're trained to size up situations, determine the risks involved, and make their own safety the first priority when deciding if they should try to rescue others.

In this module, you'll learn about practices and techniques that CERTs use during search and rescue operations. Following these practices helps keep both rescuers and survivors safe in the wake of a disaster.

It should take you about **1 hour 15 minutes** to complete the three lessons in this module:

- Lesson 5-1: Introduction to Light Search and Rescue — **30 minutes**
- Lesson 5-2: Search Operations — **15 minutes**
- Lesson 5-3: Rescue Operations — **30 minutes**

After completing this module, you should be able to:

- Identify practices that CERTs must follow during search and rescue operations

Lesson Overview

Welcome to Lesson 5-1: Introduction to Light Search and Rescue.

In this lesson, you'll learn about key principles and practices for light search and rescue. Chief among these principles is rescuer safety, including special sizeup issues that apply to search and rescue operations.

After completing this lesson you should be able to:

- Identify CERT practices for light search and rescue
- Identify sizeup issues for CERT search and rescue operations

It should take about **30 minutes** to complete this lesson.

Components of Search and Rescue

CERT search and rescue has three interdependent components:

- Sizeup
- Search Operations
- Rescue Operations

The first component, sizeup, is the information-gathering and decision-making process for determining whether to attempt a rescue and, if so, how to proceed.

As you're doing a search and rescue sizeup, you need to keep in mind that the most important person in a rescue attempt is …

You — the rescuer — are the most important person in a rescue attempt.

And performing an effective sizeup is an important first step in protecting yourself.

Remember the nine steps of the basic sizeup process:

- Step 1: Gather facts
- Step 2: Assess and communicate damage
- Step 3: Consider probabilities
- Step 4: Assess your situation
- Step 5: Establish priorities
- Step 6: Make decisions
- Step 7: Develop action plans
- Step 8: Take action
- Step 9: Evaluate progress

Later in this lesson, we'll focus specifically on sizeup as it is applied to light search and rescue.

Search operations are the second component in the process. To locate potential survivors, you need to use search techniques that:

- Protect your safety
- Are systematic and thorough
- Avoid duplication of efforts

Lesson 5-2: Search Operations will introduce safe and effective search methods and discuss how to document your search.

Rescue operations are the third component that comes into play after sizeup and search operations have taken place. Rescue involves three main functions:

- Creating a safe environment
- Triaging or stabilizing survivors

- Removing survivors

Lesson 5-3: Rescue Operations will introduce methods such as leveraging and cribbing to create a safe environment and discuss techniques for removing survivors based on their condition, resource availability, and stability of the environment.

Knowledge Review

A CERT will be doing light search and rescue following a flood. What is the team's first priority when it's conducting the search and rescue operations?

    A. Making sure that all survivors are located
    B. Avoiding property damage
    C. CERT member safety
    D. Minimizing time in the structure

Answer:
C

Knowledge Review

Suppose that you're a member of a CERT that's performing light search and rescue in a residential area that has been damaged by a windstorm. Why should you complete a sizeup before you enter a house to search for survivors?

    A. To see if there are fatalities outside that should be addressed first
    B. To determine whether to attempt a rescue and how to proceed
    C. To decide how many CERT members should be on each search and rescue team
    D. To calculate how long CERT members can stay in the structure

Answer:
B

Rescuer Safety

Regardless of the severity of structural damage, rescuer safety is always a CERT's primary concern during search and rescue operations.

The two most frequent causes of rescuer deaths are:

- Disorientation (rescuers become disoriented after entering a structure and lose their way)
- Secondary collapse (all or part of the structure collapses after the rescuers have entered)

Bearing these facts in mind, CERT rescuers perform only light search and rescue; they avoid heavily damaged structures. They also follow four essential safety practices to protect themselves.

Safe Practices

Safe Practice 1: Use Protective Equipment

Always wear personal protective equipment (PPE), including:

- Heavy work gloves
- Goggles
- Dust mask
- Helmet
- Sturdy shoes or boots

The primary cause of rescuer problems after working in a structural collapse is from breathing dust. A dust mask is **essential**!

Dust mask: *The best type of dust mask is an N95, which will filter particles as small as 3 microns. Dust masks won't filter chemical or biological agents. If chemical or biological agents are suspected to be present, evacuate to an upwind location and notify first responders.*

Safe Practice 2: Work as a Team

Successful search and rescue depends on teamwork! When performing search and rescue:

- **Use a buddy system**. Always work in pairs and have a third person available to act as a runner.
- **Have backup teams available**. Having backup teams allows teams to rotate, prevents fatigue, and makes sure that help is available if a team gets into trouble.

Remember: All teams need to take breaks, drink fluids, and eat to keep themselves fresh.

Safe Practice 3: Put Rescuer Safety First

Rescuer safety always has top priority. When considering a search and rescue attempt:

- Conduct a thorough sizeup.
- Make rescuer safety the number one priority in any decision to attempt a rescue.
- Never enter a structure that you determine has heavy damage.
- Limit the amount of time that CERTs spend in moderately damaged buildings.
- Never search an area that's covered by water.

Safe Practice 4: Be Alert for Hazards

Sizeup is an ongoing process. Look up, down, and all around for safety hazards. Before you enter a building, evaluate its exterior from all sides. Once inside, constantly re-evaluate the situation to identify hazards and changing conditions that could compromise your safety, such as:

- Power lines
- Natural gas leaks
- Hazardous materials
- Sharp objects
- Overhead objects that could fall
- Holes in flooring
- Water
- Smoke

Knowledge Review

Select True or False for each of the following statements to indicate what search procedures and rescue operations CERTs must follow.

1. T   F   Wear personal protective equipment at all times

2. T   F   Rescue heavily trapped survivors first

3. T   F   Avoid searching in areas with standing water

4. T   F   Enter heavily damaged buildings only after doing a careful sizeup

5. T   F   Consider their own safety first

6. T   F   Perform a sizeup before deciding whether to attempt a rescue

7. T   F   Assign one person per rescue to preserve team resources

Answer

    1. T
    2. F
    3. T
    4. F
    5. T
    6. T
    7. F

Search and Rescue Operations Sizeup

Sizeup is an essential component of many CERT procedures. In this lesson, we'll focus specifically on the nine steps of sizeup as they relate to search and rescue.

Sizeup Step 1: Gather Facts

Before you can make a damage assessment, you need to gather the critical facts about the situation. You need to consider the following factors, all of which have the potential to affect search and rescue operations:

- Time of day and the day of the week when the event occurred
- Type of structure involved
- Whether the structure is occupied
- Weather conditions following the event
- Hazards that may be present

Sizeup Step 2: Assess and Communicate Damage

Damage may be:

- Light
- Moderate
- Heavy

The CERT mission changes according to the level of structural damage. Your classroom training in the *CERT Basic Training* course will cover this information more specifically for hazards in your area.

Sizeup Step 3: Consider Probabilities

During sizeup, you need to consider what probably will — or could — happen. Identify potentially life-threatening hazards. Think about:

- How stable is the situation?
- What else could go wrong?

- How would these probabilities, if they occurred, affect search and rescue operations?

Sizeup Step 4: Assess Your Situation

The next step is to assess your situation, drawing on everything you learned in the previous sizeup steps. Your assessment should determine:

- Whether the situation is safe enough to continue
- The risks faced by rescuers if they continue
- Resource requirements for safely conducting the operation
- Resource availability

Resource: Resources for search and rescue include personnel, equipment, and tools, such as those used for lifting, moving, and cutting disaster debris.

Sizeup Steps 5 and 6:
Establish Priorities and Make Decisions

Next, prioritize and make decisions about the tasks before you. You should be guided by:

- The underlying CERT priorities
- Your team's evaluation of the current situation

Deploy resources to do the most good while ensuring CERT member safety.

Do tasks that involve removing known dangers before beginning the search or the rescue. For example, turn off leaking gas from outside the building BEFORE searching the building.

Sizeup Step 7: Develop Action Plans

During this step, the Team Leader will decide specifically how personnel and other resources will be deployed and how the team will proceed with the search and rescue operation.

Because incidents requiring search and rescue operations are often somewhat complex, it may be helpful to develop a simple written plan. Written notes can help focus the operation and will provide documentation that your team can share with responding agencies.

Sizeup Steps 8 and 9:
Take Action and Evaluate Progress

Sizeup is a continual process. As the search and rescue team takes action, it needs to do ongoing evaluation to maintain a safe environment.

In turn, the information gained through evaluation needs to be fed back into the decision-making process, so that priorities and action plans can be revised when needed.

Knowledge Review

Place the nine steps of the sizeup process for search and rescue in the proper order.

____Develop action plans
____Consider probabilities
____Assess your situation
____Establish priorities
____Assess damage
____Make decisions
____Take action
____Gather facts
____Evaluate progress

Answer:
7, 3, 4, 5, 2, 6, 8, 1, and 9

Knowledge Review

A natural gas explosion that occurred in a restaurant in a shopping center has caused different levels of damage to several buildings. The restaurant and the two stores on either side of it are heavily damaged; a sporting goods store several doors down is moderately damaged; and a clothing store that's across the street from the restaurant is lightly damaged. Which of these structures might a CERT enter to search for survivors, after completing a sizeup? Select all that apply.

   A. The restaurant
   B. The two stores on either side of the restaurant
   C. The sporting goods store
   D. The clothing store

Answer:
C and D

Lesson Summary

In this lesson, you learned about fundamental principles and practices that CERTs must follow to carry out search and rescue operations safely.

Key points covered in this lesson include:

- CERT search and rescue includes initial sizeup, search operations, and rescue operations.
- The goals of CERT search and rescue are to protect rescuer safety and to rescue as many survivors as possible as quickly as possible.
- Search and rescue teams protect rescuer safety by wearing personal protective equipment, working as a team, putting rescuer safety first, doing ongoing sizeup, and remaining alert to changing situations.

REMEMBER! This training does NOT prepare you to perform CERT functions. Proper CERT training requires classroom-based instruction and supervised practice.

You've completed this lesson. You're now ready to begin Lesson 5-2: Search Operations.

Module 5: Search and Rescue
Lesson 5-1: Search Operations

Lesson Overview

Welcome to Lesson 5-2: Search Operations.

In this lesson, you'll learn about practices that CERTs use to conduct search operations safely.

After completing this lesson you should be able to:

- Identify effective methods for conducting search operations
- Identify effective methods for interior search

Later, when you take the classroom *CERT Basic Training* course, you'll be trained in how to actually **perform** these techniques.

It should take you about **15 minutes** to complete this lesson.

Search Sizeup

The first step in a search is to conduct a sizeup of the building to determine if the structure has light, moderate, or heavy damage. During this sizeup process, you:

- Gather more information about occupancy and danger (how many people may be inside, hazardous materials that may be present, etc.)
- Correct outside problems (turn off gas if there is a leak, etc.)
- Determine if you'll enter the building
- Determine a plan of action for the search, if it's safe to enter the building

As part of your sizeup, you may need to talk to bystanders or people who are familiar with the structure to obtain information that will help you plan effectively.

Bear in mind, though, that bystanders may be confused by the disorienting nature of the event. They may exaggerate numbers or may have inaccurate memories of what's happened.

Search Methodology

Search operations involve using an effective search methodology, based on the sizeup, to locate potential survivors.

An effective search methodology:

- Is systematic and thorough
- Avoids unnecessary duplication of efforts
- Documents search results

The classroom-based *CERT Basic Training* course will provide you with detailed information on the various search methods that CERTs use and will give you opportunities to practice the different methods.

For now, we'll briefly review four basic methods for locating survivors and documenting results.

Call Out to Survivors

After completing your sizeup and determining it's safe to begin search operations, start by calling out to survivors.

- Shout something such as, "If anyone can hear me, come to the sound of my voice." Repeat the call a number of times to allow survivors to locate you and respond.
- If any survivors respond, give them further directions, such as "Stay here" or "Wait outside," depending on the condition of the building.
- Ask the responding survivors for any information that they may have about the building or about other survivors who may be trapped.
- Periodically stop all movement and listen for sounds of trapped survivors.

Use a Systematic Search Pattern

To make sure that all areas of the building are covered, search the area systematically, using a consistent search pattern, such as bottom-up/top-down or right-wall/left-wall.

Following a pattern is very important in poorly lit areas. If you must leave the building, turn around and reverse your search to get back to your starting point.

For example, for a systematic right-wall room search, use your right hand to follow the wall throughout the building. If it becomes necessary to leave the area before the search is completed, turn around and use your left hand to follow the wall back to your starting point.

A right-wall or left-wall search can work equally well. The important thing is for everyone on the search team to know what pattern will be used.

Knowledge Review

After doing sizeup and determining it's safe to go ahead, a CERT enters a lightly damaged building to search for survivors. What should the CERT members do to begin locating survivors?

    A. Shoot a flare into the building to let survivors know that help has arrived
    B. Move directly to the building's exit and then work their way back
    C. Assign each CERT member a specific area to search
    D. Call out to ask survivors who can walk to come to the sound of their voices

Answer:
D

Knowledge Review

A CERT will be doing search and rescue in a lightly damaged three-story office building. What would be an example of a common systematic search pattern the team might use? Select all that apply.

    A. Right-wall or left-wall
    B. Over-and-out
    C. Bottom-up or top-down
    D. Spiral triangulation
    E. Through-and-through

Answer:
A and C

Mark Searched Areas

Search and rescue teams should use a marking system to:

- Show that a team has entered a building

- Prevent duplication of search efforts
- Document the results of the team's search when it leaves the building

You'll learn local marking protocols for your area during the *CERT Basic Training* course.

Report Results

Finally, CERTs should keep complete records of their search and rescue operations, including information about:

- Removed survivors
- People who remain trapped or are dead and their locations

CERTs should report this information to emergency services personnel when those personnel reach the disaster scene.

Knowledge Review

A CERT that's doing search and rescue finds that another CERT has put these markings directly on the exterior of a building. What do the markings indicate? Select all the answers that apply.

A. A team has entered the building
B. Other CERTs do not need to search the building
C. Documentation of the first CERT's search results
D. Verification that OSHA search regulations have been met

Answer:
A, B, and C

Knowledge Review

You've carefully maintained records of the search and rescue operation that your CERT has just completed. What should you do with these records?

A. Retain them for protection against future liability
B. Send them to your local CERT Coordinator

C. Provide them to emergency services personnel when they arrive on the scene
D. Destroy them immediately after all the survivors have been rescued

Answer:
C

Lesson Summary

In this lesson, you learned some of the effective methods for safely searching the interior of structures that may have been damaged during a disaster.

Key points covered in this lesson include:

- Search operations should begin with a sizeup of the exterior of the building or structure.
- Effective search methods include calling out, using a systematic search pattern, marking searched areas, and reporting results.

REMEMBER: This training does NOT prepare you to perform CERT functions. Proper CERT training requires classroom-based instruction and supervised practice.

You've completed this lesson. You're now ready to begin Lesson 5-3: Rescue Operations.

Module 5: Search and Rescue
Lesson 5-3: Rescue Operations

Lesson Overview

Welcome to Lesson 5-3: Rescue Operations.

In this lesson, you'll learn about key procedures for safely conducting rescue operations.

After completing this lesson you should be able to:

- Identify safe techniques for debris removal and survivor

extraction. It should take you about **30 minutes** to complete this

lesson.

Creating a Safe Environment

Two major efforts in rescue operations involve moving debris and moving survivors. To protect themselves so they can accomplish their mission, rescuers need to create a safe environment by:

- Following standard safety precautions
- Using proper techniques for moving debris and survivors

In this lesson, we'll review the precautions that apply and introduce you to some of the techniques that CERTs use during search and rescue. Later, when you take the classroom *CERT Basic Training* course, you'll be trained in how to actually **perform** these techniques.

Working Within Your Limits

Volunteers have been injured or killed because they didn't pay attention to their physical limitations and their levels of mental fatigue.

During lengthy search and rescue operations, it's important to take breaks to:

- Eat
- Drink fluids
- Rest and relax

Taking care of yourself in this way prepares you to return to the rescue effort with a clearer mind and improved energy.

Using Personal Protective Equipment

ALWAYS use the proper safety equipment for the situation, including:

- Heavy work gloves
- Goggles
- Dust mask
- Helmet
- Sturdy shoes or boots

Following Safety Procedures

During rescue operations, follow established basic safety procedures at all times. These include:

- Work in pairs — never alone.
- Never enter a building with heavy damage, because it's considered an unstable structure. Mark the building to indicate that it's unsafe to enter and then leave immediately.
- Don't try to lift or carry more than is reasonable for you.
- Use proper lifting techniques.
- Carry loads close to the body.

Proper Lifting Techniques

Wait a minute. Refresh my memory. What are the proper techniques for lifting?

To lift safely:

- Bend your knees
- Keep your back straight
- Push up with your legs

Knowledge Review

Teresa is helping her fellow CERT members remove debris during a search and rescue operation. This requires lifting various objects. What should she do to lift the objects safely? Select all the answers that apply.

    A. Hold the lifted object as far from her body as she can
    B. Bend her knees as she lifts an object
    C. Keep her back straight as she lifts an object
    D. Push up with her legs as she lifts an object

Answer:
B, C, and D

Leveraging and Cribbing

Leveraging and cribbing are two techniques that CERT members use together when they have to lift a heavy object to free a survivor who's pinned beneath the object.

Leveraging is using a lever and fulcrum to move a heavy object. A lever can be a pry bar, a sturdy piece of lumber, or another long, sturdy tool. The fulcrum is the axis point that the lever is placed against.

Cribbing is placing stabilizing material under the lifted edge of the object. Cribbing helps to stabilize fallen material and can be used to create a fulcrum for leveraging.

Leveraging and cribbing is a multi-step process that begins with leveraging.

Step 1: Place a stationary object under the lever to act as a fulcrum.

Step 2: Using the fulcrum, wedge the lever under the object that you need to move.

Step 3: Force the end of the lever down on the fulcrum. This action lifts the wedge end under the object, raising the object.

At this point, cribbing comes into play.

Step 4: Raise the object slowly, and stabilize it with cribbing material as you go. Follow the principle of "lift an inch; crib an inch." Alternately, lift the object and place cribbing materials under the lifted edge to stabilize it. Do this gradually, both for stability and to make the job easier. Be careful to keep your hands and feet out from under the object that's being lifted.

Step 5: When sufficient lift has been achieved, remove the survivor from beneath the object. What do you think needs to be done to finish the job safely?

After you've removed the survivor, slowly lower the raised object by reversing the leveraging and cribbing process. Lever the object and remove one layer of cribbing material at a time until the object is down and stable. Never leave an unsafe condition!

Leveraging, cribbing, and survivor removal is a labor-intensive and time-consuming process. It requires at least five CERT members, and each member of the team plays a specific role in the process.

You'll learn the details of how team members work together to perform leveraging and cribbing in the classroom *CERT Basic Training* course. For now, simply bear in mind that CERTs should remove lightly trapped survivors first, before attempting to free survivors whose rescue will require leveraging and cribbing.

Debris Removal

In some situations, to locate survivors you'll need to remove lighter debris. This doesn't require leveraging and cribbing, but you must still be careful to remove the debris safely. Set up a human chain and pass the debris from one CERT member to the next. Be sure to set up the chain in a position that won't interfere with rescue operations. And don't forget to wear leather work gloves to protect your hands!

Knowledge Review

After first rescuing lightly trapped survivors from an office building, a CERT will attempt to free a survivor who is pinned beneath a fallen cabinet. What technique should the team use to lift the cabinet?

    A. Human chain
    B. Cribbing
    C. Stabilizing
    D. Leveraging
    E. Triaging

Answer:
D

Knowledge Review

A CERT will need to use leveraging and cribbing to free a survivor whose leg is trapped beneath a fallen beam in a damaged house. Which of the following are key safety principles that the team should follow as it performs the rescue?

    A. Lift from the waist, not the knees
    B. Keep hands and feet out from under the object that's being lifted
    C. Always keep the survivor's head elevated during the lift
    D. Lift an inch; crib an inch
    E. Lower the lifted object after removing the survivor

Answer:
B, D, E

Selecting the Survivor Removal Method

You need to take several factors into account when deciding on the best method for removing a survivor.

General stability of the immediate environment: In a structure with light damage, injured survivors should be treated on site by the medical team. In a moderately damaged building, the survivor should be removed as quickly as possible, using a method that's safe for the rescuers and the survivor given the amount of debris and available space.

Number of rescuers available: You can use a variety of techniques to move survivors, depending on how many rescuers can assist. These include one-person and two- person carries, and other carries that require more rescuers to move a survivor.

Strength and ability of the rescuers: Don't attempt to lift more than is reasonable for your size and strength. The one-person arm carry is reserved for a small survivor carried by a physically able rescuer. The distance to be covered should also be considered. Your safety is the number one priority, so opt out of any carry that you're not physically able to do.

Condition of the survivor: Physically able survivors can assist in their own removal. If safety and time permit, a survivor with a suspected closed-head or spinal injury should not be lifted or dragged. If removal is necessary, take every precaution to keep the survivor's spine in a straight line, using a backboard before removing the survivor.

Removing Survivors

When removing survivors, rescuers must use teamwork and communication among everyone involved in the lift. This is important for rescuer and survivor safety.

You can use a variety of techniques to remove survivors, including:

- Self-removal or assist
- One-person carries
- Two-person carries
- Group carries
- Dragging

We'll briefly review these methods now. Later, when you take the *CERT Basic Training* classroom course, you'll see demonstrations of each method and have opportunities to practice them.

Self-Removal or Assist

It's usually best to allow survivors who are capable of freeing themselves to do so. However, seemingly able-bodied survivors are sometimes weaker and more injured than they think. When survivors are freed, they may need your assistance to exit the structure.

One-Person Carry

The one-person carry should be used only if the survivor is small and you're physically able to carry the person over the required distance to get to safety.

Two-Person Carry

Survivor removal is easier when multiple rescuers are available. With the two-person carry, the person lifting the survivor's feet can face either toward or away from the survivor.

A chair carry is another type of two-person carry. If a sturdy chair is available, two rescuers can seat the survivor on the chair and carry the seated survivor to safety.

Group Carry

A blanket carry, in which a blanket or similar material serves as an improvised stretcher, is an example of a group carry. Six rescuers are recommended for a blanket carry to help make sure that the survivor remains stable during the move. One rescuer must be designated the lead person to ensure teamwork when performing the lift.

Dragging

If there's no other way to remove a survivor from a confined area, you can drag the survivor on a blanket or by the survivor's shoulders or feet.

This method should be used only when it's time-critical to remove the survivor from the structure and no other removal method is available. Do not drag a survivor when debris could cause additional injury.

Knowledge Review

A CERT will be rescuing survivors from a store that has been moderately damaged by a storm. Several survivors are still in the store, but they're not severely injured and they are able to walk. Which of the following would be the best removal technique for the CERT to use to rescue these relatively able-bodied survivors?

    A. Triaged assist with leveraging
    B. Chair carry with cribbing assist
    C. Two-person carry
    D. Self-removal with assistance to exit the structure
    E. Blanket carry with at least five rescuers for each survivor

Answer:
D

Knowledge Review

In which of the following situations is a one-person carry most likely to be an appropriate method of removing the primary survivors of the disaster? Select all that apply.

    A. The roof has collapsed on a factory; the primary survivors are all adults.
    B. A preschool has been damaged by a flood; the primary survivors are
       all children under the age of 5.

C. A college dormitory has been damaged by a fire; the primary survivors are all college students between the ages of 18 and 22.
D. A church has been hit by a tornado during a religious service; the primary survivors include adults of all ages, teenagers, and small children and infants.

Answer:
B and D

Search and Rescue Scenario

A hurricane recently hit a coastal city. Wind and rain have caused damage across the area. The hurricane changed paths and was stronger than expected, catching office workers off guard. A local CERT has been activated to search for the survivors.

Scenario Question 1

The team surveys the buildings in the area to determine which one is safe for them to search. Read the descriptions below and select which on you think the CERT could safely search?

A. Building with entire first floor collapsed
B. Building surrounded by water with a lot of water inside
C. Building with debris but little visible damage

Answer:
C

Scenario Question 2

Before the CERT members begin their search, they discuss the safety precautions they should take. What safety precautions do you think the team should take?

A. Wear personal protective equipment at all times.
B. Enter heavily damaged buildings only after a careful sizeup.

C. Assign one person per search and rescue to preserve team resources.
D. Conduct a sizeup before entering any building.

Answer:
B and D

Scenario Question 3

The team has begun its search using a proper search methodology. In what order should the following search methods be done?

____Report results of search.
____Use a systematic search pattern.
____Call out to survivors.
____Mark entrance to searched areas to indicate search activities.

Answer:
3, 2, 1, 4

Scenario Question 4

After calling out for survivors, the CERT members think they hear someone, but they aren't sure. They begin a search pattern to sweep the house. Which of the following statements concerning search patterns is true?

   A. The team should use a search pattern only if the house is poorly lit.
   B. The team should use a bottom-up or top-down pattern and a right-wall or left-wall pattern.
   C. The team should use a right-wall or left-wall pattern only if it plans to leave the same way it entered.

Answer:
B

Scenario Question 5

The first person the CERT come to is Beverly, who is trapped under a couch. Beverly is conscious and in good spirits. She has some pain and may be injured. She is talkative and just wants to get herself and her co-workers out of the building. Should the CERT members attempt this rescue?

A. Yes
B. No

Answer:
A

Scenario Question 6

The couch is removed, and Beverly is no longer trapped. She is alert, with a bruised and possibly sprained ankle and a sore back. The room is stable, and several other CERT members have arrived. How should the CERT members remove her?

A. A blanket carry, since they have at least six people.
B. Dragging method, since she has a hurt leg.
C. Self-removal, as long as her leg isn't broken.

Answer:
A

Scenario Question 7

George is also trapped. He is in a back office where a portion of the ceiling has collapsed on him. George is conscious but having trouble breathing and thinks his leg may be broken. Should the CERT members attempt this rescue?

A. Yes
B. No

Answer:
B

Scenario Question 8

Christina is also trapped, in another office. She's surrounded by light debris, mainly the contents of a bookcase and some rubble. She is conscious and talking and is more shocked than physically injured. Should the CERT members attempt this rescue?

A. Yes
B. No

Answer:
A

Scenario Question 9

Since Christina is trapped only by light debris, the team will set up a human chain to remove the debris around her. Which of the following are true about debris removal? Select all that apply.

    A. Use a human chain only if you have fewer than five people.
    B. Wear leather work gloves to protect hands.
    C. Set up the chain away from rescue operations.
    D. Remove all debris from room before conducting rescue.
    E. Hand off debris from one person to the next.

Answer:
B, C, and E

Scenario Question 10

After the CERT members have removed the debris, they are ready to remove Christina. She doesn't appear to have any injuries and is just a little dazed. The room is stable, and four CERT members are with her. They have to walk through two more rooms to move her to safety. One of the rooms has not been cleared of debris. Which of the following removal methods could be used with Christina?

    A. Two-person carry
    B. Blanket carry
    C. Self-removal and assist
    D. One-person carry
    E. Dragging

Answer:
C

Scenario Question 11

Once a building is searched and survivors are removed, the CERT members should prepare to mark the building and report their findings. Is the following statement true or false: Mark a building only if survivors were found and a rescue took place.

A. True
B. False

Answer:
B

Lesson Summary

In this lesson, you learned about key procedures CERTs follow for safely conducting rescue operations.

Key points covered in this lesson include:

- The goals of rescue operations are to maintain rescuer safety and rescue survivors as quickly as possible while minimizing additional injury to them.
- Rescuers can create a safe environment by:
    o Working within their limits
    o Using personal protective equipment
    o Following safety procedures
    o Using leveraging and cribbing to move and stabilize debris
    o Using safe methods to remove survivors

You've completed this lesson.

CAUTION!!

Although you've completed this lesson on search and rescue, you haven't been trained to perform CERT functions. Only the classroom-based *CERT Basic Training* course provides the instruction and supervised practice that are required to do leveraging, cribbing, and survivor removal safely.

Do **NOT** try to use the procedures introduced in this lesson until you have completed the CERT classroom training on search and rescue.

Now let's review what you learned in this module and find out what you can expect to learn in the next module.

Module Summary

In Module 5: Search and Rescue, you learned about practices that CERTs use to carry out search and rescue operations safely.

Key points that were covered include:

- CERT search and rescue includes initial sizeup, search operations, and rescue operations.
- The goals of CERT search and rescue are to protect rescuer safety and to rescue as many survivors as possible as quickly as possible.
- Search and rescue teams protect rescuer safety by wearing personal protective equipment, working as a team, putting rescuer safety first, doing ongoing sizeup, and remaining alert to changing situations.
- Search operations should begin with a sizeup of the exterior and interior of the building or structure.
- Effective search methods include calling out, using a systematic search pattern, marking searched areas, and reporting results.
- The goals of rescue operations are to maintain rescuer safety and rescue survivors as quickly as possible while minimizing additional injury to them.
- Rescuers can create a safe environment by:
    - Working within their limits
    - Using personal protective equipment
    - Following safety procedures
    - Using leveraging and cribbing to move and stabilize debris
    - Using safe methods to remove survivors

What's Next?

Now that you've completed this module, you're ready to move on to Module 6: Course Summary. In that module, you'll review the main concepts that we've covered in this training and prepare for the end-of-course test. You'll also find out what you need to do to take the test, print your completion certificate, and go on to take the classroom-based *CERT Basic Training* course.

Module 6: Course Summary
Lesson 6-1: Finishing Up

Module Overview

In this module, you'll review the main concepts that were covered in the first five modules in this course:

- Module 1: CERT Basics
- Module 2: Fire Safety
- Module 3: Hazardous Materials and Terrorist Incidents
- Module 4: Disaster Medical Operations
- Module 5: Search and Rescue

You'll also find out about printing your completion certificate for this course and going on to take the classroom-based *CERT Basic Training* course that's required for you to become a trained and qualified CERT member.

It should take you about **20 minutes** to complete this module. After you've done that, you should be ready to take the final exam for this training.

Module 1 Review

Module 1: CERT Basics

- When disaster overwhelms emergency response resources, CERTs can extend the capabilities of response organizations through hazard mitigation and response activities.
- Before disaster strikes, you should mitigate potential hazards in the home and workplace, develop a family emergency plan, and assemble a disaster supply kit.
- Obtaining the maximum benefit from CERT response activities requires a carefully structured CERT organization. CERT decision-making is guided by the goal of protecting team members' safety while doing the greatest good for the greatest number of people.

Module 2 Review

Module 2: Fire Safety

- Fire requires heat, fuel, and oxygen. Take away any one of these elements, and fire can't be sustained.
- The type of fuel dictates both the class of fire (A, B, C, D, K) and the best methods and equipment for extinguishing a fire.
- A CERT member's fire safety role begins with mitigating fire hazards related to electricity, natural gas, and flammable liquids at home and in the workplace.
- Suppressing small fires is one of the CERT roles. The decision to extinguish a fire is based on personal safety and having the proper resources.

When suppressing fires, CERT members guard their safety by:

- Wearing protective equipment
- Working as a team
- Planning for safe entry and exit
- Maintaining a safe distance and position in relation to the fire
- Suppressing only small fires, using the proper equipment
- Using the PASS procedure to operate fire extinguishers
- Overhauling the fire to prevent re-ignition

The sizeup process includes the following steps:

1. Gather facts
2. Assess and communicate the damage
3. Consider probabilities
4. Assess your own situation
5. Establish priorities
6. Make decisions
7. Develop plans of action
8. Take action
9. Evaluate progress

Module 3 Review

Module 3: Hazardous Materials and Terrorist Incidents

The best way to protect yourself from household chemical emergencies is to practice LIES:

- **L**imit the amount of hazardous materials in storage.
- **I**solate products in approved containers and protect them from sources of ignition.

- **E**liminate products that are no longer necessary by disposing of them properly.
- **S**eparate incompatible materials.

Hazardous materials:

- The NFPA 704 Diamond identifies hazardous materials stored at fixed facilities.
- When a facility is placarded with an NFPA 704 Diamond, the only action that CERT members should take during disaster response is to evacuate persons who are downwind to an uphill and upwind location.
- The DOT placard system is used to identify hazardous materials in transit in the United States.

Terrorist Incidents:

- Terrorist incidents may involve chemical or biological materials, dirty bombs, nuclear blasts, conventional explosives, and other weapons.
- Safety for all CERT members and persons in the area of a terrorist incident is of first concern.
- Terrorist incident sites are crime scenes, and care must be taken to protect evidence. Leave all items alone unless moving something is absolutely necessary for life safety.
- Terrorist incidents are a "stop sign." If there are any indicators of a terrorist incident, do not proceed. Move away from the object or area to an uphill and upwind location and report it to authorities immediately.
- Do not use a cellular phone or two-way radio if you suspect an explosive device is present. Use a landline phone instead.
- Do not attempt to treat survivors in a contaminated area. Tell people who are leaving the area to use basic decontamination procedures and to wait for responders to perform complete decontamination.

Module 4 Review

Module 4: Disaster Medical Operations

- The conditions that always get first treatment priority include obstructed airway, excessive bleeding, and shock.
- Use direct pressure, elevation, and pressure points, as needed, to control bleeding.

Medical Treatment Areas

- Clearly marked medical treatment areas and morgues help responders efficiently treat survivors.

- Public health measures should include proper hygiene, sanitation, and water purification.
- After all survivors have been triaged and treated for the three "killers," CERT members assess each survivor from head to toe before beginning treatment of any other injuries.

The Role of the CERT Member

- CERTs provide basic treatment for common injuries, including burns, wounds, fractures/sprains, and hypothermia.
- To limit the effects of vicarious trauma, CERT members avoid over-identifying with survivors, monitor their own trauma symptoms, and use stress reduction techniques.
- When working with survivors, CERT members stabilize the incident scene by stabilizing individuals.

Module 5 Review

Module 5: Search and Rescue

- The goals of CERT search and rescue are to protect rescuer safety and to rescue as many survivors as possible as quickly as possible.
- During search and rescue, CERT members create a safe environment by:
  - Working within their limits
  - Working as a team and putting rescuer safety first
  - Using personal protective equipment
  - Remaining alert to hazards
  - Following all safety procedures
  - Moving and stabilizing debris by leveraging and cribbing
  - Using safe methods to remove survivors
- Search should begin with a sizeup of the exterior and interior of the building or structure.
- Effective search methods include calling out to survivors, using a systematic search pattern, marking searched areas, and reporting results.
- Rescue objectives are to maintain rescuer safety and to triage and evacuate survivors as quickly as possible while minimizing additional injury to them.

Lesson Summaries

Each lesson in this course included a summary of key points covered in the lesson. If you'd like to study any of these summaries before you take the final exam, select your choice:

Lesson 1-1: CERT Overview

- Disasters may overwhelm emergency response resources.
- CERTs can extend the capabilities of response organizations through hazard mitigation and response activities.
- Before a disaster, CERTs focus on emergency preparedness and hazard mitigation.
- After a disaster, CERTs may operate directly or assist responders in activities to save or sustain lives and protect property.

Lesson 1-2: Family and Workplace Preparedness

- Identify potential hazards in the home and workplace.
- Take steps to mitigate those hazards.
- Develop and practice a family disaster plan.
- Assemble a disaster supply kit.

Lesson 1-3: CERT Organization

- The ICS is used to manage emergency operations.
- CERTs use ICS, which expands and contracts as needed to handle the situation.
- Efficient two-way communication is essential for effective decision-making.
- The CERT decision-making process is guided by the goal of CERT safety.

Lesson 2-1: Introduction to Fire Safety

- Fire requires heat, fuel, and oxygen. The combination of these elements can cause a chemical exothermic reaction (fire).
- There are five classes of fire, and they are based on the type of fuel that feeds the fire.
- The type and quantity of fuel dictate the best methods and equipment for extinguishing a fire.
- The decision to extinguish a fire should be based on maintaining your personal safety and having access to the proper resources.

Lesson 2-2: Fire Hazards in the Home and Workplace

- A CERT member's fire safety role begins at home and at the workplace.
- Electricity, natural gas, and flammable liquids can create fire hazards.
- Taking the time to look for and eliminate fire hazards reduces the risk of having a fire occur in the home or workplace.

Lesson 2-3: Safe Fire Suppression

- Wear protective equipment.
- Work with a buddy and as a team.

- Plan for safe entry and exit.
- Maintain a safe distance and position in relation to the fire.
- Suppress only small fires, using the proper equipment.
- Use the PASS procedure to operate fire extinguishers.
- Overhaul the fire to prevent re-ignition.

Lesson 3-1: Introduction to Special Situations

- Treat hazardous materials as STOP signs: Only professional responders with special equipment are trained to deal with these situations.
- If you become contaminated, use basic decontamination procedures and then wait for responders to perform complete decontamination.

Lesson 3-2: Hazardous Materials Safety

- Taking the time to read product labels can reduce the chances of an accident.
- In cases of a hazardous materials emergency, you need to evaluate the type of exposure and type of chemical involved before taking action.
- The NFPA placard system is an important way to identify fixed locations where hazardous materials are used or stored.
- The DOT placard system is an important way to recognize vehicles or containers that carry hazardous materials in transit.

Lesson 3-3: Terrorism and CERT

- Personal safety is always your first priority.
- In the event of a terrorist attack, it is important to stay informed. Monitor television, radio, and Internet news broadcasts to keep on top of the situation.
- Always have a plan of action in case of terrorism. Your plan should include an emergency kit, an evacuation route, and supplies to shelter in place.

Lesson 4-1: Introduction to Disaster Medical Operations

- The CERT goal is to stay safe and do the greatest good for the greatest number of survivors.
- Trauma injuries in disasters can often result in death. Sometimes these deaths can be prevented through simple, early treatment. CERT members are trained to provide this treatment until medical professionals are available to help.
- Do not apply the medical treatment skills covered in this module until you have completed classroom *CERT Basic Training* course.

Lesson 4-2: Principles and Guidelines for Survivor Care

- The three killers - obstructed airway, excessive bleeding, and shock
- Purpose of triage

- Purpose and importance of head-to-toe assessment
- Neck, spine, and head injuries
- Common injuries, such as burns and wounds
- The purpose of medical treatment areas
- Public health concerns after disasters

Lesson 4-3: Disaster Psychology

- To limit the effects of vicarious trauma on yourself, don't over-identify with survivors. Monitor your own reactions and use stress reducers that work for you.
- Traumatic stress may affect a survivor's cognitive functioning, physical health, and interpersonal relationships.
- When working with survivors, the CERT psychological role is to stabilize the incident scene by stabilizing individuals.

Lesson 5-1: Introduction to Light Search and Rescue

- CERT search and rescue includes initial sizeup, search operations, and rescue operations.
- The goals of CERT search and rescue are to protect rescuer safety and to rescue as many survivors as possible as quickly as possible.
- Search and rescue teams protect rescuer safety by wearing personal protective equipment, working as a team, putting rescuer safety first, doing ongoing sizeup, and remaining alert to changing situations.

Lesson 5-2: Search Operations

- Search operations should begin with a sizeup of the exterior of the building or structure.
- Effective search methods include calling out, using a systematic search pattern, marking searched areas, and reporting results.

Lesson 5-3: Rescue Operations

- The goals of rescue operations are to maintain rescuer safety and rescue survivors as quickly as possible while minimizing additional injury to them.
- Rescuers can create a safe environment by:
  - Working within their limits
  - Using personal protective equipment
  - Following safety procedures
  - Using leveraging and cribbing to move and stabilize debris
  - Using safe methods to remove survivors

Limitations of Your Training

Now that you've had time to review the material covered in this training, you're nearly ready to move forward. But first a word of CAUTION!! Even though you've completed these training modules, you're not trained to perform CERT functions. Do NOT try to use any of the procedures introduced in this training until you've completed the classroom-based CERT Basic Training course. That course provides the instruction and supervised practice that are required for you to become a fully trained and qualified CERT member. At this point, however, you should be ready to take the next steps in your CERT training, which are …

Next Steps

1. Take the final exam for this training course
2. Print your completion certificate after you pass the exam
3. Take the classroom-based *CERT Basic Training* course

Taking the Final Exam

To take the final exam for this training course:

- Download and print a copy of the final exam in PDF format
  - Circle your answers on the printed exam to save time when you go online
- Complete the online answer sheet

To pass the exam, you must get at least 31 of the 40 questions on the exam correct, giving you a score of 77.5% or higher.

If you get 30 or fewer questions correct, you won't pass the exam. If you don't pass on your first try, you should review the modules where you had difficulty. Then go through Module 6: Course Summary again, in order to re-take the exam.

Printing Your Certificate

When you're notified that you've passed the exam, you'll then be able to print your completion certificate from your own computer.

Taking the *CERT Basic Training* Classroom Course

To arrange to take the CERT classroom training, go to the CERT national Web site and locate a nearby CERT training program, based on your ZIP code.

If there is no nearby CERT training program available in your area, select here to find out how to get one started.

Knowledge Review

Take a moment to think about what you've learned in this course. Based on this information, what are some changes you plan to make in your home and workplace to prepare for a disaster? Write your answers below and compare to the answers given.

____
____
____
____
____

Answer:
Here are some examples of responses that other learners have made:

- Put together a disaster plan for my family and test it
- Prepare an emergency supply kit for my office
- Install a carbon monoxide detector in the basement near the furnace
- Gather up leftover household chemicals for proper disposal
- Restock food and medical supplies at home for shelter-in-place emergency

Conclusion

Congratulations! You've completed this training course.

Once you've passed the exam, you'll receive a message with a link for the certificate. You can download the certificate to your computer and save an electronic copy before printing it out on your printer.

To take the final exam, select here.